Series/Number 07-130

D0162324

NONPARAMETRIC SIMPLE REGRESSION: SMOOTHING SCATTERPLOTS

JOHN FOX
McMaster University

SAGE PUBLICATIONS
International Educational and Professional Publisher
Thousand Oaks   London   New Delhi

For information:

Sage Publications, Inc.
2455 Teller Road
Thousand Oaks, California 91320
E-mail: order@sagepub.com

Sage Publications Ltd.
6 Bonhill Street
London EC2A 4PU
United Kingdom

Sage Publications India Pvt. Ltd.
M-32 Market
Greater Kailash I
New Delhi 110 048 India

Printed in the United States of America

Library of Congress Cataloging-in-Publication Data

Fox, John, 1947–
    Nonparametric simple regression: Smoothing scatterplots / by John Fox.
        p.   cm. — (Quantitative applications in the social sciences; v. 130)
    Includes bibliographical references.
    ISBN 0-7619-1585-0 (pbk.: acid-free paper)
    1. Regression analysis.   2. Nonparametric statistics.   I. Title.   II. Sage
university papers series. Qantitative applications in the social sciences; v. 130.

QA278.2 .F62 2000
519.5'36—dc21   99-049870

This book is printed on acid-free paper

    01   02   03   04   05   06   7   6   5   4   3   2

Acquiring Editor:	C. Deborah Laughton
Editorial Assistant:	Eileen Carr
Production Editor:	Diana Axelsen
Production Assistant:	Cindy Bear

When citing a university paper, please use the proper form. Remember to cite the Sage University Paper series title and include the paper number. One of the following formats can be adapted (depending on the style manual used):

(1) FOX, J. (2000) *Nonparametric Simple Regression: Smoothing Scatterplots.* Sage University Papers Series on Quantitative Applications in the Social Sciences, 07-130. Thousand Oaks, CA: Sage.

OR

(2) Fox, J. (2000). *Nonparametric Simple Regression: Smoothing Scatterplots.* (Sage University Papers Series on Quantitative Applications in the Social Sciences, series no. 07-130). Thousand Oaks, CA: Sage.

CONTENTS

---

*Sections marked by an asterisk contain more difficult material. See page 8 for details.

ACKNOWLEDGMENTS

I am grateful to two anonymous reviewers, to Michael Lewis-Beck, the editor of the QASS series, and to Scott Long for helpful comments on a draft of this monograph. I also wish to thank Deborah Laughton, my editor at Sage, for her encouragement and support.

SERIES EDITOR'S INTRODUCTION

In analyzing the relationship between two quantitative variables, the first thing we should do is look at the scatterplot. This visual assessment helps us judge functional form. Suppose Professor Gwen Greene, a political scientist, is studying the link between a nation's population size (x), and its number of elected officials (y), in a sample of 94 nations. Her particular research question concerns the shape of association. Is it linear or is it something else? Unfortunately, the scatterplot is not clear. The point cloud is just that, a cloud of points with no apparent geometry. A common response is to impose linearity and to estimate the relationship with ordinary least squares regression (OLS), but she knows that strategy can go badly wrong. The relationship might in fact be curvilinear, meaning the OLS result would be biased from specification error. How do we find that curve? One approach is to deduce it from theory and prior research, model it, for example, perhaps it is a quadratic equation, and estimate. However, imagine that in the research at hand theory and prior research give contradictory guidance. Then another approach is to explore the data systematically to uncover the curve, if it exists. This latter strategy leads to nonparametric simple regression techniques, which Professor Fox so ably explicates here.

Nonparametric regression does not assume x and y relate in a particular function form. Rather, employing the sample data, it calculates different average y values, for grouped x values. These average y values are smoothed, like dots connected by lines, into a curve. That curve, which may be wavy, wiggly, or otherwise irregular, represents in a refined way the functional relationship between the two variables. When the scatterplot is "smoothed" in this manner, the method generally used is some version of locally weighted regression, "loess," for short.

Since the search for form is inductive, many curves are possible. The shape of the curve depends on bin definition, the method of averaging, or the order of the local polynomial regression. Other technical issues involve kernel estimation, outlier treatment, and oversmoothing. In particular, as much "art" as "science" is involved in ensuring that the curves are neither "too smooth" nor "too rough." Once a curve is arrived at, a confidence envelope may be constructed around it, and hypotheses tests can be carried out.

One drawback is that nonparametric regression, as the name implies, yields no regression parameter estimates. However, identification of the proper functional form, made possible by the method, may lead to a general theoretical model specification that yields unbiased parameter estimates. For example, say Professor Greene finds a loess smooth curve between nation population (x) and elected officials (y), where, as x increases, y increases less and less. The suggestion is that the relationship is logarithmic, and might be expressed by transformation in an OLS equation, where y is a function of log x. Thus, the smoothing exercise made for the discovery of a deeper functional form that can be subjected to further testing. This theory building role emerges out of Professor Fox's last chapter, where he relates the general issue of nonlinearity to nonparametric regression. In general, this carefully crafted monograph follows the venerable tradition of inductive science. It reminds us that thoughtful data exploration can teach us a great deal.

—Michael S. Lewis-Beck
Series Editor

For Jesse and Bonnie

NONPARAMETRIC REGRESSION ANALYSIS: SMOOTHING SCATTERPLOTS

JOHN FOX
McMaster University

1. WHAT IS NONPARAMETRIC REGRESSION?

Regression analysis traces the average value of a response variable (y) as a function of one or several predictors (xs). Suppose that there are two predictors, x_1 and x_2. Denote the population mean value of y conditional on the predictors (i.e., fixing the predictors at specific values x_1 and x_2) as $\mu \mid x_1, x_2$. Then the central object of regression analysis is to estimate the *population regression function* $\mu \mid x_1, x_2 = f(x_1, x_2)$ on the basis of sample data. Alternatively, we may focus on some other aspect of the conditional distribution of y given the xs, such as the median value of y or the standard deviation of y.

As it is usually practiced, regression analysis assumes a linear relationship of y to the xs, so that

$$\mu \mid x_1, x_2 = f(x_1, x_2) = \alpha + \beta_1 x_1 + \beta_2 x_2$$

or, alternatively and equivalently, that

$$y = \alpha + \beta_1 x_1 + \beta_2 x_2 + \varepsilon,$$

where the average value of the "error" ε is 0. It is also typically assumed, at least implicitly, that the conditional distribution of y is, except for its mean, everywhere the same and that this distribution is a normal distribution,

$$y \sim N(\alpha + \beta_1 x_1 + \beta_2 x_2, \sigma^2),$$

or, equivalently, that the errors are normally distributed with constant variance, $\varepsilon \sim N(0, \sigma^2)$. Finally, it is assumed that observations are

1

sampled independently, so the y_i and $y_{i'}$ (or equivalently, ε_i and $\varepsilon_{i'}$) are independent for $i \neq i'$. The full suite of assumptions leads to the commonly applied method of linear least squares regression.

These are strong assumptions and there are many ways in which they can go wrong: For example, as is typically the case in time-series data, the errors may not be independent, or the conditional variance of y (the "error variance") may not be constant, or the conditional distribution of y may be substantially nonnormal—heavy-tailed or skewed.

Nonparametric regression analysis relaxes the assumption of linearity, substituting the much weaker assumption of a smooth population regression function $f(x_1, x_2)$. The cost of relaxing the assumption of linearity is substantially greater computation and, in some instances, a more difficult-to-understand result. The gain is potentially a more accurate estimate of the regression function. Indeed, in some applications, a blind assumption of linearity can lead to meaningless results.

Some might object to the apparently "atheoretical" character of nonparametric regression, which does not attempt to specify the form of the regression function $f(x_1, x_2)$ in advance of examination of the data. I believe that this objection is ill-considered: Social theory might suggest that y depends on x_1 and x_2, but it is exceedingly unlikely to tell us that the relationship is linear. A necessary, if not sufficient, condition of effective statistical data analysis is for statistical models to summarize the data accurately.

This monograph takes up nonparametric *simple* regression, where there is a quantitative response variable y and a single predictor x, so $y = f(x) + \varepsilon$. A companion monograph (Fox, in press) describes *generalized nonparametric regression* models—for example, for a dichotomous (two-category) response variable—and nonparametric *multiple* regression—where there are several predictors.

At first blush, nonparametric simple regression may not appear to be of much use, because most interesting applications of regression analysis employ several predictors. Nevertheless, nonparametric simple regression is useful for two reasons:

1. Nonparametric simple regression is often called *scatterplot smoothing*, because in typical applications, the method passes a smooth curve through the points in a scatterplot of y against x. Scatterplots are (or should be) omnipresent in statistical data analysis and presentation,

both in the preliminary examination of regression data and in the examination of diagnostic plots derived from a regression analysis (see Chapter 7).

2. Nonparametric simple regression forms the basis, by extension, for nonparametric multiple regression and directly supplies the building blocks for a particular kind of nonparametric multiple regression called *additive regression* (see Fox, in press, and the occupational prestige example in the next section).

1.1. Preliminary Examples

1.1.1. Infant Mortality

As mentioned, an important application of nonparametric regression is to scatterplot smoothing. Figure 1.1(a) shows the relationship between infant-mortality rates (infant deaths per 1000 live births) and gross domestic product (GDP) per capita (in U.S. dollars) for 193 nations of the world. The data come from the United Nations (1998) and the example was inspired by Leinhardt and Wasserman (1978), who drew a similar graph for data collected around 1970. The nonparametric regression line on the graph was produced by a method called *lowess*. Lowess (also rendered *loess*) is an implementation of local polynomial regression, described in Section 4.4. It is the most commonly available method of nonparametric regression.

Although infant mortality declines with GDP, the relationship between the two variables is highly nonlinear: As GDP increases, infant mortality initially drops steeply, before nearly leveling out at higher levels of GDP. Because both infant mortality and GDP are highly skewed, most of the data congregate in the lower-left corner of the plot, making it difficult to discern the relationship between the two variables. The linear least squares fit to the data does a poor job of describing this relationship.

In Figure 1.1(b), both infant mortality and GDP are transformed by taking logs. Now the relationship between the two variables is nearly linear. Transformations for linearity are discussed in Chapter 7.

1.1.2. Married Women's Labor-Force Participation

Generalized nonparametric regression (described in the companion monograph, Fox, in press) is the nonparametric analog of the generalized linear model (McCullagh & Nelder, 1989). An important ap-

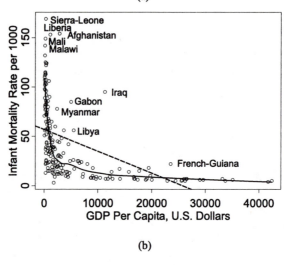

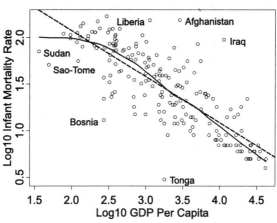

Figure 1.1. Infant-mortality rate per 1000 and GDP per capita (in U.S. dollars) for 193 nations. The straight line in each panel is a linear least squares fit to the data; the curve is estimated by local linear nonparametric regression. A few apparently unusual observations are labeled. The data are graphed on the original scales in panel (a) and on log scales in panel (b).

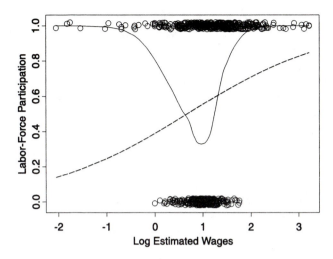

Figure 1.2. Scatterplot of labor-force participation (1 = yes, 0 = no) by the log of estimated wages. The points are vertically jittered to minimize over-plotting. The broken line shows the fit of a linear logistic regression; the solid line shows the fit of a nonparametric logistic regression.

plication is to binary data. Figure 1.2 shows the relationship between married women's labor-force participation and the log of the women's "expected" (i.e., estimated) wage rate. The data, from the 1976 U.S. Panel Study of Income Dynamics, were originally employed by Mroz (1987), and were used by Berndt (1991) as an exercise in linear logistic regression and by Long (1997) to illustrate that method. Because the response variable is discrete, taking on only two values, I have "jittered" the points in the scatterplot by adding a small random quantity to each vertical coordinate. Otherwise, many of the points would be overplotted and the graph would be less informative. Even with jittering, it is hard to discern the relationship between the two variables, but the nonparametric logistic-regression line shown on the plot reveals that the relationship is curvilinear. The linear logistic-regression fit, also shown, is misleading.[1]

1.1.3. Prestige of Canadian Occupations

Blishen and McRoberts (1976) reported a linear multiple regression of the rated prestige of 102 Canadian occupations on the income and education levels of these occupations in the 1971 Canadian census. The purpose of this regression was to produce substitute predicated prestige scores for many other occupations for which income and education levels were known, but for which direct prestige ratings were unavailable. Figure 1.3 shows the results of fitting an additive nonparametric regression to Blishen's data. As the name implies, the additive nonparametric regression model assumes that y is an additive, but not necessarily linear, function of the predictors,

$$y = \alpha + f_1(x_1) + f_2(x_2) + \varepsilon.$$

The graphs in Figure 1.3 show the estimated partial regression functions for income $\widehat{f_1}$ and education $\widehat{f_2}$. The function for income is substantially nonlinear; that for education is somewhat less so. This example is developed in Fox (in press) and in Chapter 7.

1.2. Plan of This Monograph

- Nonparametric regression is essentially a simple idea, and Chapter 2 describes simple approaches to the regression problem based on *binning* (categorization) and *local averaging*.
- Chapter 3 extends the idea of local averages to locally weighted averages, called *kernel estimates*.
- In Chapter 4, local averaging is generalized to *local linear and polynomial regression*, the core method described in this monograph.
- Chapter 5 presents approximate methods of statistical inference for local regression.
- Chapter 6 describes *smoothing splines*, an alternative method of nonparametric regression, and compares this approach to kernel and local-polynomial estimators.
- The routine application of nonparametric regression in data analysis is the subject of Chapter 7.

1.3. Notes on Background, Approach, and Computing

I assume that readers are familiar with linear least squares multiple regression and that they have been exposed to the essential ideas of statistical inference, including the notions of bias and variance in estimation.

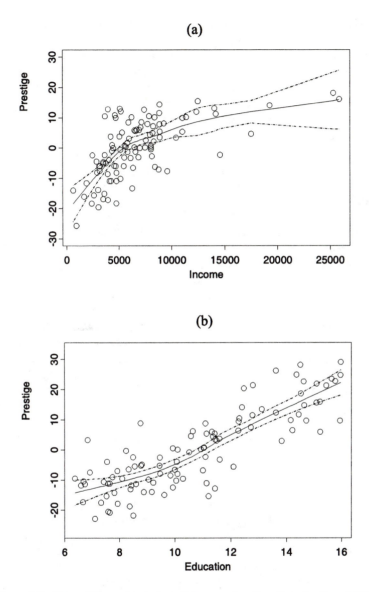

Figure 1.3. Plots of the estimated partial-regression functions for the additive regression of prestige on the income and education levels of 102 occupations. The points in the graphs represent "partial residuals" (see Chapter 7) for each predictor. The broken lines give pointwise 95% confidence envelopes.

My goal is to write a broadly accessible account of nonparametric regression, without unduly watering down the subject. To this end, I have segregated more difficult material in sections denoted by an asterisk. The asterisked material employs calculus or matrix notation, or involves a relatively intricate argument.

Rather than present an encyclopedia of methods for nonparametric regression, I concentrate on local polynomial estimation, which is the most widely available and commonly used method, although Chapter 6 also describes a competing technique, *smoothing splines*. Statistical theory, insofar as it is introduced, is treated informally and only to illuminate the rationale for and use of nonparametric regression in data analysis.

Readers who are convinced of the utility of nonparametric regression analysis will naturally (I hope) want to employ it in their work. Here I have both good and disappointing news: At the time of writing, lowess scatterplot smoothing is available in most of the major statistical computer packages, but more general and advanced methods of nonparametric regression analysis (as described here and in Fox, in press), including methods for statistical inference, are not. An exception is the S statistical computing environment (described, e.g., in Venables & Ripley, 1997), which is particularly strong in its nonparametric-regression capabilities. S is distributed commercially as S-Plus; a work-alike called R is available as freeware. Further information on computing, along with the data sets employed in this monograph and internet links, may be found on my web site, a link to which is provided at the Sage website ⟨http://www.sagepub.com⟩; search for "John Fox." I will endeavor to keep the information on my web site up to date.

2. BINNING AND LOCAL AVERAGING

Suppose that the predictor variable x is discrete—that is, x takes on a limited number of separate values. For concreteness, let x be age at last birthday and let y be income in dollars. We want to know how the average value of y (or, perhaps, some other characteristics of the distribution of y) changes with x; that is, we want to know $\mu \,|\, x$ for each value of x. Given data on the entire population, we can calculate these conditional population means directly. If we have a

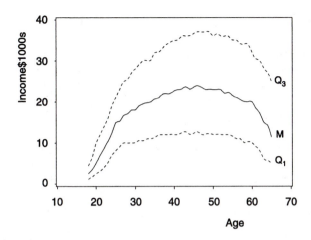

Figure 2.1. Simple nonparametric regression of income on age, with data from the 1990 U.S. Census one-percent sample. The solid line, marked M, is the median income conditional on age; the broken lines marked Q_1 and Q_3 are, respectively, the first and third quartiles of the conditional distributions of income given age.

very large sample, then it is still easy to accomplish our goal: Simply calculate the sample average income for each value of age, $\bar{y} \mid x$; in a very large sample, the estimates $\bar{y} \mid x$ will be close to the population means $\mu \mid x$. Alternatively, we could focus on conditional quantiles of the distribution of income given age, such as the median and quartiles.

Figure 2.1, for example, shows the median and quartiles of the distribution of income from wages and salaries as a function of single years of age. The data are taken from the 1990 U.S. Census One-Percent Public Use Microdata Sample and they represent a total of 1.24 million observations. Because the distribution of income conditional on age is positively skewed (and very high incomes are censored) and because the conditional variance of income is not constant, it is more informative to graph quantiles of the distribution than to calculate and graph the conditional mean.

2.1. Binning

Now suppose that the predictor variable x is continuous (or practically so). Instead of age at last birthday, for example, we have each individual's age to the minute. Even in a very large sample, there will be very few individuals of precisely the same age, and conditional sample averages $\bar{y} \mid x$ would, therefore, each be based only on one observation or at best a few observations. Consequently, these averages would be highly variable and would be poor estimates of the population means $\mu \mid x$; moreover, many exact ages would not even be observed, leaving us without estimates of $\mu \mid x$.

Because we have a very large sample, however, we can dissect the range of x into a large number of narrow class intervals or *bins*. Each bin, for example, could constitute age rounded to the nearest year (returning us to single years of age). Let $x_1, x_2, \ldots, x_b$ represent the x values at the bin centers. Each bin contains a lot of data and, consequently, the conditional sample averages, $\bar{y}_i = \bar{y} \mid (x \text{ in bin } i)$, are very stable. Because each bin is narrow, these bin averages do a good job of estimating the regression function $\mu \mid x$ anywhere in the bin, including at its center.

Given sufficient data, there is essentially no cost to binning, but in smaller samples, it is not practical to dissect the range of x into a large number of narrow bins: There will be few observations in each bin, making the sample bin averages $\bar{y}_i$ unstable. To calculate stable averages, we need to use a relatively small number of wider bins, producing a cruder estimate of the population regression function.

There are two obvious ways to proceed: (1) We could dissect the range of x into bins of equal width. (2) We could dissect the range of x into bins containing roughly equal numbers of observations. The first option is attractive only if x is sufficiently uniformly distributed to produce stable bin averages based on a sufficiently large number of observations. Indeed, if we pursue this option in a small sample, we may end up with some empty bins.

Figure 2.2 depicts the binning estimator applied to the U.N. infant-mortality data introduced in Chapter 1. The line in this graph employs 10 bins, each with roughly 19 observations. Because the predictor variable GDP is highly skewed, 10 equal-width bins would not be appropriate here: The first bin would contain 131 of the 193 observations, while the last would contain only two observations.

Treating a discrete quantitative predictor variable as a set of categories and binning continuous predictor variables are common strategies in the analysis of large data sets. Often, continuous variables are implicitly binned in the process of data collection, as in a sample sur-

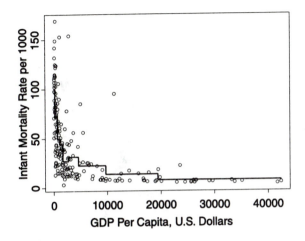

Figure 2.2. The binning estimator applied to the relationship between infant mortality per 1000 and GDP per capita, in U.S. dollars. Ten bins are employed.

vey that asks respondents to report income in class intervals (e.g., $0 to $4999, $5000 to $9999, $10,000 to $14,999, etc.). If there are sufficient data to produce precise estimates, then using dummy variables for the values of a discrete predictor or for the class intervals of a binned predictor is preferable to blindly assuming linearity. An even better solution is to compare linear and nonparametric specifications (see Section 5.2).

2.1.1. Statistical Considerations*

A narrow bin is depicted in Figure 2.3(a); the data represent the whole population within the bin. The population average value of y in the bin, $\overline{\mu}_i = E(y \mid x$ in bin $i)$, is nearly the same as the population conditional average at the center of the bin, $\mu_i = \mu \mid x_i$, or indeed anywhere in the bin. In a very large sample, the bin sample mean $\overline{y}_i = \overline{y} \mid (x$ in bin $i)$ will, therefore, provide a precise estimate of $\mu \mid x$ anywhere in the bin.

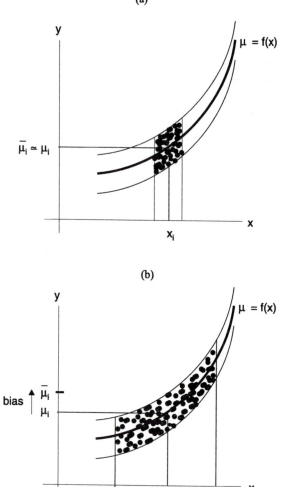

Figure 2.3. When the bin is narrow, as in (a), the population average y in the bin, $\bar{\mu}_i$, is nearly equal to the level of the regression curve at the center of the bin, μ_i, even though the regression is nonlinear. When the bin is wide, as in (b), the population average in the bin $\bar{\mu}_i$ generally differs from the level of the regression curve at the center of the bin μ_i. Note that the spread of the data around the regression curve (the vertical separation of the lines) is constant: the lines *appear* to converge only because their slope is increasing.

Now consider what happens if we make the bin wide, as in Figure 2.3(b):

- Unless a happy accident has occurred, the population bin average $\overline{\mu}_i = E(y \,|\, x$ in bin $i)$ and the conditional average value μ_i of y at the center of the bin will be different.
- Suppose that we want to estimate $\mu \,|\, x$ at some *focal point* x_0 in bin i based on sample data. The sample bin average $\overline{y}_i$ is an unbiased estimator of the population bin average $\overline{\mu}_i$, but because $\overline{\mu}_i$ generally differs from $\mu \,|\, x_0$ (even at the center of the bin), $\widehat{f}(x_0) = \overline{y}_i$ is a biased estimator of the regression function $\mu \,|\, x_0 = f(x_0)$. By definition, the bias at x_0 is $\overline{\mu}_i - \mu \,|\, x_0$.
- Because we would like the bias to be small, we prefer narrows bins, but unless we have a lot of data, narrow bins mean little data contributing to each sample average $\overline{y}_i$, producing highly variable sample averages. The mean-squared error of estimation is the sum of squared bias and sampling variance:

$$\mathrm{MSE}\!\left[\widehat{f}(x_0)\right] = \mathrm{bias}^2\!\left[\widehat{f}(x_0)\right] + V\!\left[\widehat{f}(x_0)\right].$$

As is frequently the case in statistical estimation, minimizing bias and minimizing variance work at cross-purposes: Wide bins produce small variance and large bias; narrow bins produce large variance and small bias. Only if we have a very large sample can we have our cake and eat it too. All methods of nonparametric regression bump up against this problem in one form or another.

- Even though the binning estimator is biased, it is *consistent* as long as the population regression function is reasonably smooth. All we need do is shrink the bin width to 0 as the sample size n grows, but shrink it sufficiently slowly that the number of observations in each bin grows as well. Under these circumstances, bias$[\widehat{f}(x)] \to 0$ and $V[\widehat{f}(x)] \to 0$ as $n \to \infty$.

2.2. Local Averaging

The essential idea behind *local averaging* is that, as long as the regression function is smooth, observations with x values near a focal x_0 are informative about $f(x_0)$. Local averaging is very much like binning, except that rather than dissecting the data into nonoverlapping bins, we move a bin (called a *window*) continuously over the data, averaging the observations that fall in the window.

It is not possible in practice to estimate the regression function at an infinite number of x values, but we can calculate $\widehat{f}(x)$ at a large number of focal values of x, usually equally spread within the range of observed x values, or at the observations, $x_{(1)}, x_{(2)}, \ldots, x_{(n)}$. (The parenthetical subscripts indicate that the x values are arranged in ascending order.[2])

As in binning, we can employ a window of fixed width w centered on the focal value x_0, or we can adjust the width of the window to include a constant number of observations, m. These are the *m nearest neighbors* of the focal value.

Problems occur near the extremes of the xs. For example, all of the nearest neighbors of $x_{(1)}$ are greater than or equal to $x_{(1)}$, and the nearest neighbors of $x_{(2)}$ are almost surely the same as those of $x_{(1)}$, producing an artificial flattening of the estimated regression curve at the extreme left, called *boundary bias*. A similar flattening occurs at the extreme right, near $x_{(n)}$. One solution is to require equal numbers of neighbors to the right and left of the focal value, but such *symmetric neighborhoods* necessarily have decreasing numbers of observations as we approach the boundary of the data, so that (in the absence of tied values at the boundary) the only observation in the neighborhood of $x_{(1)}$ is $x_{(1)}$ itself. A better solution to boundary bias is described in Chapter 4 on local regression.

Figure 2.4 shows how local averaging works using the relationship of prestige to income in the Canadian occupational prestige data introduced in Chapter 1. The window shown in panel (a) of the figure includes the $m = 40$ nearest neighbors of $x_{(80)}$. Having identified the nearest neighbors of the focal x, the y values associated with these observations are averaged, producing the fitted value $\widehat{y}_{(80)}$ in panel (b). Fitted values are calculated for each focal x (in this case $x_{(1)}, x_{(2)}, \ldots, x_{(102)}$) and then connected, as in panel (c). In addition to the obvious flattening of the regression curve at the left and right, local averages are rough, because $\widehat{f}(x)$ tends to take small jumps as observations enter and exit the window. The kernel estimator, described in Chapter 3, produces a smoother result. Finally, local averages are subject to distortion when outliers fall in the window, a problem addressed in Section 4.4.

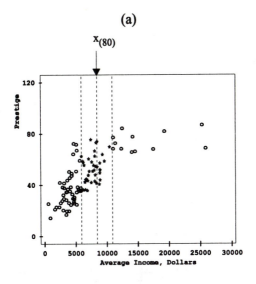

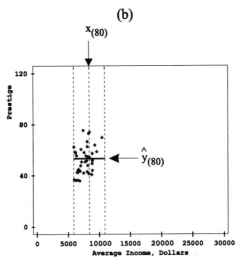

Figure 2.4. Nonparametric regression of prestige on income using local averages: (a) A window is defined to enclose the $m = 40$ nearest x neighbors of the focal value $x_{(80)}$. (b) The mean y-value is computed for the 40 observations in the window, producing $\widehat{y}_{(80)}$. This procedure is repeated for windows centered on each of the $n = 102$ x values. (c) The nonparametric regression line connects the 102 averaged y values.

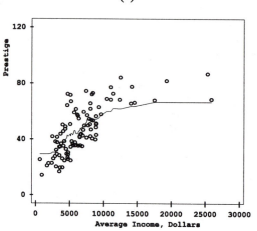

Figure 2.4. Continued.

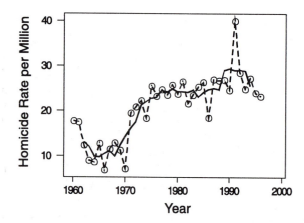

Figure 2.5. Homicide rate per million population for Metropolitan Toronto, 1960 to 1996. The observed homicide rates are given by the circles connected by a broken line. The solid line shows a five-point moving average.

2.2.1. Moving Averages for Time-Series Data

A common and long-standing application of nonparametric regression is to time-series data, where the x variable is time and the observations are equally spaced. In this context, nearest-neighbor and fixed-width windows are identical. Local averages applied to time-series data are often called *moving averages*.

Figure 2.5, for example, shows the annual homicide rate per million population for Metropolitan Toronto for the years 1960 through 1996. Moving averages are shown for successive groups of $m = 5$ observations. Because the first three moving averages are necessarily identical, $\widehat{f}(1960)$ and $\widehat{f}(1961)$ are not shown; $\widehat{f}(1995)$ and $\widehat{f}(1996)$ are omitted for a similar reason.

There are many variations on moving averages, including methods based on medians and schemes for producing estimates at the boundaries (see, e.g., Tukey, 1977, chap. 7). Because the general methods of nonparametric regression described in this monograph work quite well for time-series data, however, I shall not describe these specialized techniques. Some additional considerations that arise in the analysis of time-series data are discussed in Section 4.6, however.

3. KERNEL ESTIMATION

Kernel estimation (locally weighted averaging) is an extension of local averaging. The essential idea is that in estimating $f(x_0)$, it is desirable to give greater weight to observations that are close to the focal x_0 and less weight to those that are remote. Let $z_i = (x_i - x_0)/h$ denote the scaled, signed distance between the x value for the ith observation and the focal x_0. As I shall explain shortly, the scale factor h, called the *bandwidth* of the kernel estimator, plays a role similar to the window width of a local average.

We need a *kernel function* $K(z)$ that attaches the greatest weight to observations that are close to the focal x_0 and then falls off symmetrically and smoothly as $|z|$ grows. Given these characteristics, the specific choice of a kernel function is not critical. Having calculated weights $w_i = K[(x_i - x_0)/h]$, we proceed to compute a fitted value at x_0 by weighted local averaging of the ys:

$$\widehat{f}(x_0) = \widehat{y} \,|\, x_0 = \frac{\sum_{i=1}^{n} w_i y_i}{\sum_{i=1}^{n} w_i}.$$

18

Two popular choices of kernel functions, illustrated in Figure 3.1, are the *Gaussian* or *normal kernel* and the *tricube kernel*:

- The normal kernel is simply the standard normal density function,

$$K_N(z) = \frac{1}{\sqrt{2\pi}} e^{-z^2/2}.$$

Here, the bandwidth h is the standard deviation of a normal distribution centered at x_0. Observations at distances greater than $2h$ from the focal value therefore receive nearly 0 weight, because the normal density is small beyond 2 standard deviations from the mean.

- The tricube kernel is

$$K_T(z) = \begin{cases} (1 - |z|^3)^3 & \text{for } |z| < 1, \\ 0 & \text{for } |z| \geq 1. \end{cases}$$

For the tricube kernel, h is the half-width of a window centered at the focal x_0. Observations that fall outside of the window receive 0 weight.

- Using a *rectangular kernel* (also shown in Figure 3.1)

$$K_R(z) = \begin{cases} 1 & \text{for } |z| < 1, \\ 0 & \text{for } |z| \geq 1, \end{cases}$$

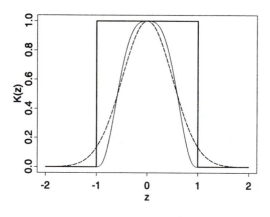

Figure 3.1. Tricube (light solid line), normal (broken line), and rectangular (heavy solid line) kernel functions. The normal kernel is rescaled to facilitate comparison.

gives equal weight to each observation in a window of half-width h centered at x_0 and, therefore, produces an *unweighted* local average, as described in Section 2.2.

I have implicitly assumed that the bandwidth h is fixed, but the kernel estimator is easily adapted to nearest-neighbor bandwidths. The adaptation is simplest for kernel functions, like the tricube kernel, that fall to 0: Simply adjust $h(x)$ so that a fixed number of observations m are included in the window. The fraction m/n is called the *span* of the kernel smoother. As in the case of local averaging, it is common to evaluate the kernel estimator either at a number of values evenly distributed across the range of x or at the ordered observations $x_{(i)}$.

Kernel estimation is illustrated in Figure 3.2 for the Canadian occupational prestige data. Panel (a) shows a neighborhood containing 40 observations centered on the 80th ordered x value. Panel (b) shows the tricube weight function defined on the window; the bandwidth $h[x_{(80)}]$ is selected so that the window accommodates the 40 nearest neighbors of the focal $x_{(80)}$. Thus, the span of the smoother is $40/102 \simeq 0.4$. Panel (c) shows the locally weighted average, $\widehat{y}_{(80)} = \widehat{y} \mid x_{(80)}$; note that this is the fitted value associated with $x_{(80)}$, *not* the 80th ordered fitted value. Finally, panel (d) connects the fitted values to obtain the kernel estimate of the regression of prestige on income. In comparison with the local-average regression (Figure 2.4), the kernel estimate is smoother, but it still exhibits flattening at the boundaries.

Varying the bandwidth of the kernel estimator controls the smoothness of the estimated regression function: Larger bandwidths produce smoother results. Choice of bandwidth is discussed in more detail in connection with local polynomial regression in Sections 4.1 and 4.3.

4. LOCAL POLYNOMIAL REGRESSION

Local polynomial regression corrects some of the deficiencies of kernel estimation. It provides a generally adequate method of nonparametric regression that extends straightforwardly to multiple regression, additive regression, and generalized nonparametric regression (as described in Fox, in press). An implementation of local polynomial regression called *lowess* (or *loess*) is the most commonly available

(a)

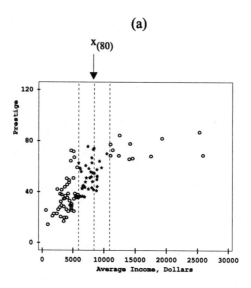

(b)

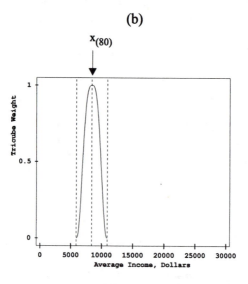

Figure 3.2. The kernel estimator applied to the Canadian occupational prestige data: (a) a window containing the $m = 40$ nearest x neighbors of the focal value $x_{(80)}$; (b) the tricube weight function; (c) the weighted average $\widehat{y}_{(80)}$ of the y values in the window; (d) the nonparametric regression line connecting the locally weighted averages centered at each x value.

(c)

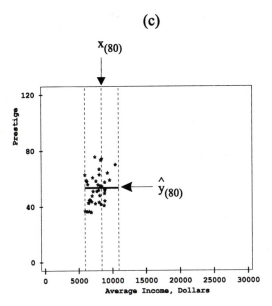

(d)

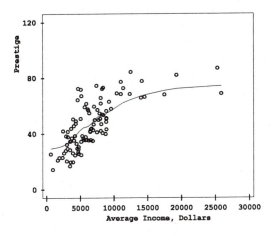

Figure 3.2. Continued.

method of nonparametric regression. For these reasons, I emphasize local polynomial regression in this monograph, and this is, therefore, the central chapter.

Perhaps you are familiar with polynomial regression, where a p-degree polynomial in a predictor x,

$$y = \alpha + \beta_1 x + \beta_2 x^2 + \cdots + \beta_p x^p + \varepsilon,$$

is fitted to data, usually by the method of least squares; $p = 1$ corresponds to a linear fit, $p = 2$ to a quadratic fit, and so. Fitting a constant (i.e., the mean) corresponds to $p = 0$.

Local polynomial regression extends kernel estimation to a polynomial fit at the focal point x_0, using local kernel weights, $w_i = K[(x_i - x_0)/h]$. The resulting weighted least squares (WLS) regression fits the equation

$$y_i = a + b_1(x_i - x_0) + b_2(x_i - x_0)^2 + \cdots + b_p(x_i - x_0)^p + e_i$$

to minimize the weighted residual sum of squares, $\sum_{i=1}^{n} w_i^2 e_i^2$. Once the WLS solution is obtained, the fitted value at the focal x_0 is just $\hat{y} | x_0 = a$. As in kernel estimation, this procedure is repeated for representative focal values of x or at the observations x_i.

The bandwidth h can be either fixed or can vary as a function of the focal x. When the bandwidth defines a window of nearest neighbors, as is the case for tricube weights, it is convenient to specify the degree of smoothing by the proportion of observations included in the window. This fraction s is called the *span* of the local-regression smoother. The number of observations included in each window is then $m = [sn]$, where the square brackets denote rounding to the nearest whole number.

Selecting $p = 1$ produces a local-linear fit, the most common case. The "tilt" of the local-linear fit promises reduced bias in comparison with the kernel estimator of the previous section, which corresponds to $p = 0$. This advantage is most apparent at the boundaries, where the kernel estimator tends to flatten. The values $p = 2$ or $p = 3$, local quadratic or cubic fits, produce more flexible regressions. Greater flexibility has the potential to reduce bias further, but flexibility also entails the cost of greater variation. There is, it turns out, a theoretical advantage to odd-order local polynomials, so $p = 1$ is generally preferred to $p = 0$, and $p = 3$ to $p = 2$. These issues are explored in Sections 4.2 and 4.3.

Figure 4.1 illustrates the computation of a local linear regression fit to the Canadian occupational prestige data, using the tricube kernel function and nearest-neighbor bandwidths. Panel (a) shows a window corresponding to a span of 0.4, accommodating the $[0.4 \times 102] = 40$ nearest neighbors of the focal value $x_{(80)}$. Panel (b) shows the tricube weight function defined on this window. The locally weighted linear fit appears in panel (c). Fitted values calculated at each observed x are connected in panel (d). There is no flattening of the fitted regression function, as there was for kernel estimation (cf. Figure 3.2).

4.1. Selecting the Span

I assume nearest-neighbor bandwidths, so bandwidth choice is equivalent to selecting the span of the local-regression smoother. I also assume a locally linear fit. The methods of this section generalize in an obvious manner to fixed-bandwidth and higher-order polynomial smoothers.

A generally effective approach to selecting the span is guided trial and error. The span $s = 0.5$ is often a good point of departure. If the fitted regression looks too rough, then try increasing the span; if it looks smooth, then see if the span can be decreased without making the fit too rough. We want the *smallest* value of s that provides a smooth fit.

The terms "smooth" and "rough" are admittedly subjective, and a sense of what I mean here is probably best conveyed by example. An illustration, for the Canadian occupational prestige data, appears in Figure 4.2. For these data, selecting $s = 0.5$ or $s = 0.7$ appears to provide a reasonable compromise between smoothness and fidelity to the data.

A complementary visual approach is to find the residuals from the fit, $e_i = y_i - \widehat{y}_i$, and to smooth the residuals against the predictor, x_i. If the data have been oversmoothed, then there will be a systematic relationship between the average residual and the predictor x; if the fit does not oversmooth the data, then the average residual will be approximately 0 regardless of the value of x. We seek the *largest* value of s that yields residuals that are unrelated to x. Examples are shown in Figure 4.3. Except at the right, where data are sparse because of the skew in the income scores, the average residuals for $s = 0.1$ and

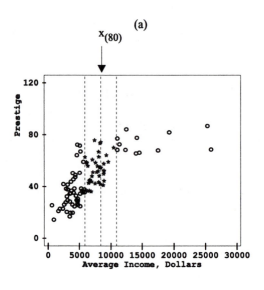

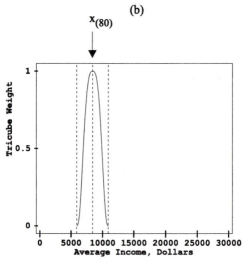

Figure 4.1. Nearest-neighbor local-linear regression of prestige on income. The window in (a) includes the $m = 40$ nearest neighbors of the focal value $x_{(80)}$. The tricube weights for this window are shown in (b), and the locally weighted least squares line is shown in (c), producing the fitted value $\hat{y}_{(80)}$. Fitted values for all of the observations are connected in (d) to produce the nonparametric regression line.

(c)

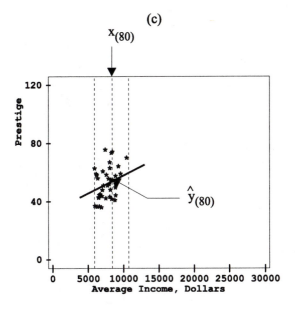

(d)

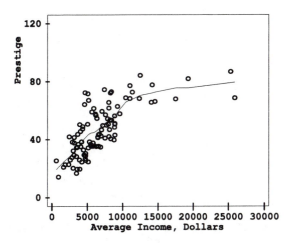

Figure 4.1. Continued.

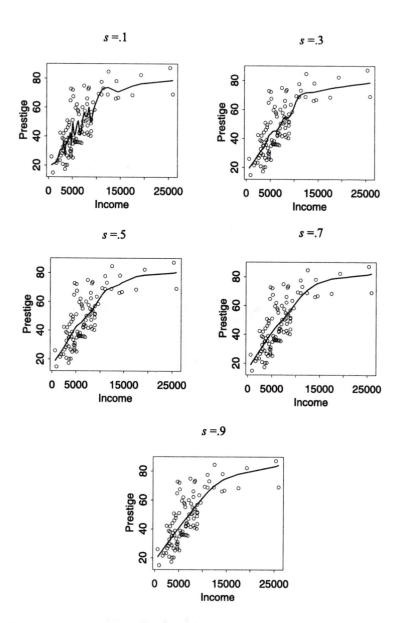

Figure 4.2. Nearest-neighbor local-linear regression of prestige on income, for several values of the span s. The values $s = 0.5$ or 0.7 appear to reasonably balance smoothness with fidelity to the data.

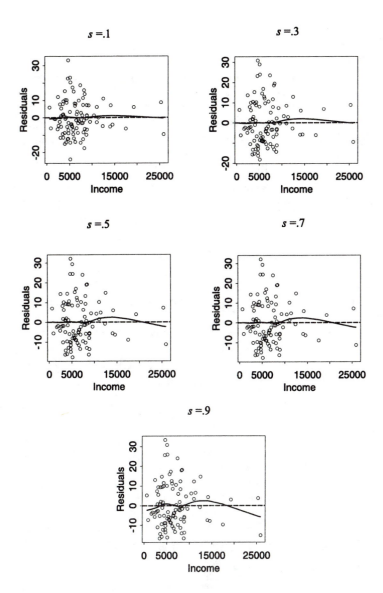

Figure 4.3. Plots of residuals against income. The horizontal line on each plot is drawn at $e = 0$; the smooth curve is calculated by local-linear regression (using span $s = 0.6$). The spans shown at the top of each plot are for the original fits from which the residuals were obtained.

$s = 0.3$ follow the 0 line very closely, the average residuals for $s = 0.5$ and $s = 0.7$ depart slightly from 0, and the residuals for $s = 0.9$ show more systematic departures from 0, indicative of oversmoothing. Combining this information with direct visual inspection of the fits in Figure 4.2 suggests picking $s \simeq 0.6$.

This kind of visual experimentation is facilitated by a computing environment that permits control of the span through a graphical device such as a slide bar. We can then adjust the span and immediately see the effect.

More sophisticated methods for selecting the span are discussed in Section 4.3.1. The visual approach usually works very well, however, and visual trial and error should be performed even if more sophisticated approaches are used to provide an initial value of s.

4.2. Statistical Issues in Local Regression*

I again assume local linear regression. The results in this section extend to local polynomial fits of higher degree, but the linear case is simpler.

Figure 4.4 demonstrates why the locally linear estimator has a bias advantage in comparison with the kernel estimator. In both panels (a) and (b), the true regression function (given by the heavy line) is linear in the neighborhood of the focal value x_0.

- In panel (a), the x values in the window are symmetrically distributed around the focal x_0 at the center of the window. As a consequence, the weighted average $\bar{\mu}$ of the ys in the window (or, indeed, the simple average of the ys in the window) provides an unbiased estimate of $\mu \mid x_0 = E(y \mid x_0)$; the local-regression line also provides an unbiased estimate of $\mu \mid x_0$ because it estimates the true local regression function.
- In panel (b), in contrast, there are relatively more observations at the right of the window. Because the true regression function has a positive slope in the window, the consequence is that $\bar{\mu}$ exceeds $\mu \mid x_0$—that is, the kernel estimator is biased. The local-linear regression, however, still estimates the true regression function and, therefore, provides an unbiased estimate of $\mu \mid x_0$. The boundaries are regions in which the observations are asymmetrically distributed around the focal x_0, accounting for the boundary bias of the kernel estimator, but the point is more general.

Of course, if the true regression in the window is nonlinear, then both the kernel estimate and the locally linear estimate usually will

(a)

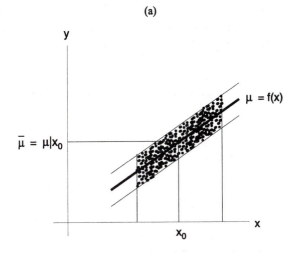

(b)

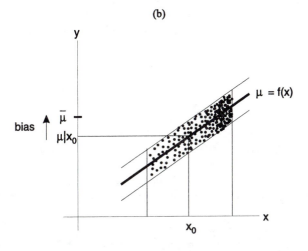

Figure 4.4. (a) When the relationship is linear in the neighborhood of the focal x_0, and the observations are symmetrically distributed around x_0, both the kernel estimator (which estimates $\bar{\mu}$) and the local-linear estimator (which, because the relationship is linear in the window, directly estimates $\mu \mid x_0$) are unbiased. (b) When the regression is linear in the neighborhood, but the observations are not symmetrically distributed around x_0, the local linear estimator is still unbiased, but the kernel estimator is biased.

be biased, though usually to varying degrees.[3] The conclusion to be drawn from these pictures is that *the bias of the kernel estimate depends on the distribution of x values, whereas the bias of the locally linear estimate does not.* Because the locally linear estimate can adapt to a "tilt" in the true regression function, it generally has smaller bias when the x values are unevenly distributed and at the boundaries of the data. Because the kernel and locally linear estimators have the same asymptotic variance, the smaller bias of the locally linear estimator translates into smaller mean-squared error.

These conclusions generalize to local polynomial regressions of even degree p and odd degree $p + 1$ (e.g., $p = 2$ and $p + 1 = 3$): Asymptotically, the bias of the odd member of the pair is independent of the distribution of x values, whereas the bias of the even member is not. The bias of the odd member of the pair is generally smaller than that of the even member, whereas the variance is the same. Asymptotically, therefore, the odd member of the pair (e.g., the local cubic estimator) has a smaller mean-squared error than the even member (e.g., the local-quadratic estimator).

I illustrate these ideas with the artificial "data" in Figure 4.5(a). I generated $n = 100$ observations according to the cubic regression equation

$$y = 100 - 5\left(\frac{x}{10} - 5\right) + \left(\frac{x}{10} - 5\right)^3 + \varepsilon, \qquad (4.1)$$

where the x values were sampled from the uniform distribution $x \sim U(0, 100)$ and the errors were sampled from the normal distribution $\varepsilon \sim N(0, 20^2)$. The line in this graph is the "true" regression curve, $E(y \mid x)$ (i.e., Equation 4.1 without the error). Figure 4.5 also shows nearest-neighbor (b) kernel and (c) locally linear fits to the data, in each case for span $s = 0.3$. The nearest-neighbor local-linear regression curve does quite a good job of recovering the true regression; the increased bias of the kernel fit is apparent, particularly near the boundaries of the data.[4]

4.3. Bandwidth Revisited*

As the bandwidth h of the local-regression estimator decreases, the bias of the estimator decreases and its variance increases. Suppose

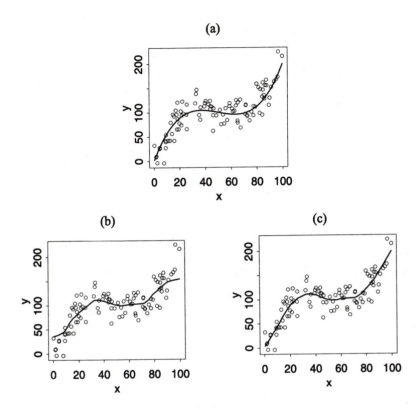

Figure 4.5. (a) Artificial data, generated according to the model $y = 100 - 5(x/10 - 5) + (x/10 - 5)^3 + \varepsilon$ with $x \sim U(0, 100)$ and $\varepsilon \sim N(0, 20^2)$. (b) The nearest-neighbor kernel fit for span $s = 0.3$. (c) The nearest-neighbor local-linear fit, again for span $s = 0.3$.

that we evaluate the local regression at the focal value x_0:

- At one extreme, $h = 0$ and only observations with x values exactly equal to x_0 contribute to the local fit. In this case, it is not possible to fit a unique local-regression line, but we could still find the fitted value at x_0 as the average y value for $x = x_0$. If there are no tied values of x_0, then the fit is exact, $\widehat{y}_0 = y_0$, and the local-regression estimator simply joins the points in the scatterplot. Because $E(y \mid x_0) = \mu \mid x_0$, the bias of the estimator is 0; its variance—equal to the conditional variance σ^2 of an individual observation—is large, however.

- At the other extreme, $h = \infty$. Then the scaled distances of predictor values x_i from the focal x_0, that is, $z_i = (x_i - x_0)/h$, are all 0, and the weights $w_i = K(z_i)$ are all equal to the maximum (e.g., 1 for the tricube kernel function). With equal weights for all of the observations, the fit is no longer local. In effect, we fit a global least squares line to the data. Now the bias is large (unless, of course, the true regression really is globally linear), but the sample-to-sample variance of the fit is small.

The bottom line is the mean-squared error (MSE) of the estimator,

$$\mathrm{MSE}(\widehat{y} \mid x_0) = E\big[(\widehat{y} \mid x_0 - \mu \mid x_0)^2\big],$$

which is the sum of variance and squared bias. We seek the bandwidth h^* at x_0 that minimizes the MSE, providing an optimal trade-off of bias against variance. Of course, we need to repeat this process at each focal value of x for which $f(x) = \mu \mid x$ is to be estimated, adjusting the bandwidth as necessary to minimize MSE.

The expectation and variance of the local-linear smoother at the focal value x_0 are

$$\begin{aligned} E(\widehat{y} \mid x_0) &\simeq f(x_0) + \frac{h^2}{2} s_K^2 f''(x_0), \\ V(\widehat{y} \mid x_0) &\simeq \frac{\sigma^2 a_K^2}{nhp(x_0)}, \end{aligned} \qquad (4.2)$$

where (as before)

- $\widehat{y} \mid x_0 = \widehat{f}(x_0)$ is the fitted value at $x = x_0$;
- $\sigma^2 = V(\varepsilon)$ is the variance of the errors, that is, the conditional variance of y around the true regression function;
- h is the bandwidth;
- n is the sample size;

and

- $f''(x_0)$ is the second derivative of the true regression function at the focal x_0 (indicative of the curvature of the regression function, that is, the rapidity with which the slope of the regression function is changing at x_0);

- $p(x_0)$ is the probability density for the distribution of x at x_0 (large values of which, therefore, indicate an x_0 near which many observations will be made);
- s_K^2 and a_K^2 are positive constants that depend on the kernel function;[5]

The bias at x_0 is

$$\text{bias}(\widehat{y} \mid x_0) = E(\widehat{y} \mid x_0) - f(x_0) \simeq \frac{h^2}{2} s_K^2 f''(x_0).$$

The bias of the estimator is large, therefore, when the bandwidth h and curvature $f''(x_0)$ of the regression function are large. In contrast, the variance of the estimator is large when the error variance σ^2 is large, when the sample size n is small, when the bandwidth h is small, and where the data are sparse [i.e., $p(x_0)$ is small].[6]

Because making h larger increases the bias but decreases the variance, bias and variance, as usual, work at cross-purposes. The value of h that minimizes the MSE—the sum of squared bias and variance—at x_0 is

$$h^*(x_0) = \left[\frac{a_K^2}{s_K^4} \times \frac{\sigma^2}{np(x_0)[f''(x_0)]^2} \right]^{1/5}, \qquad (4.3)$$

Notice that where the curvature $f''(x_0)$ is 0, the optimal bandwidth $h^*(x_0)$ is infinite, suggesting a globally linear fit to the data. Nearest-neighbor bandwidths adjust for the factor $np(x_0)$, but do not take into account the local curvature of the regression function.

Figure 4.6 illustrates these ideas for the artificial cubic regression model of the previous section. Panel (a) of the figure shows the regression function, $\mu \mid x = f(x)$ (from Equation 4.1). Panel (b) shows the variance, squared bias, and mean-squared error of $\widehat{y} \mid x$ as a function of bandwidth h at the focal value $x = 10$. Notice how the squared bias is 0 at $h = 0$ and grows as the value of h gets larger; in contrast, the variance is at its maximum at $h = 0$ and declines as the bandwidth grows. The MSE (the sum of variance and squared bias) is at a minimum at $h^*(10) \simeq 12$. Panel (c) of Figure 4.6 graphs the optimal bandwidth $h^*(x)$ as a function of the focal value x_0. Notice how $h^*(x)$ grows dramatically near $x = 50$, a point of inflection of $f(x)$, where the second derivative of the regression function is 0.

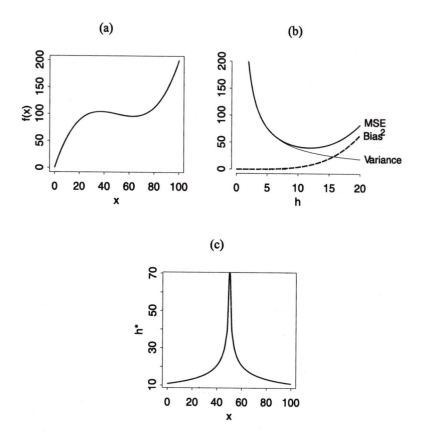

Figure 4.6. Bandwidth selection for the artificial-data illustration: (a) The true regression curve $E(y \mid x) = f(x)$. (b) The variance, squared bias, and MSE of the local-linear estimator as a function of bandwidth h at the focal value $x = 10$. (c) Optimal bandwidth h^* as a function of the focal value x; note that h^* becomes infinite at $x = 50$, since $f''(50) = 0$.

Nearest-neighbor regression adjusts the bandwidth at each focal x, but only by applying a fixed span. Figure 4.7 extends the previous example, using the artificially generated data of Equation 4.1. The local-linear fits in Figure 4.7 are for nearest-neighbor bandwidths, employing the tricube kernel function. The span of the local regression is manipulated over several values, from 0.1 to 0.9. Both the estimated regression function (shown as a solid line) and the true population

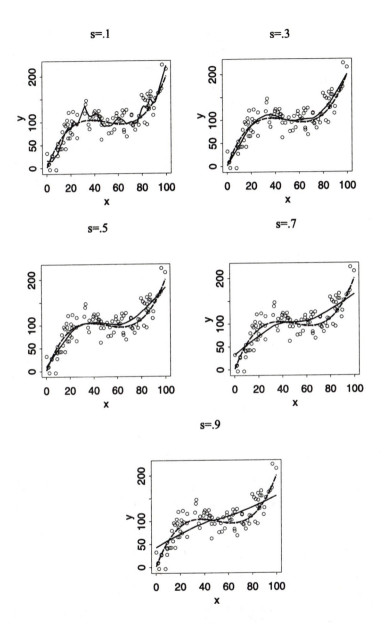

Figure 4.7. Local-linear regressions for several different spans, from $s = 0.1$ to $s = 0.9$. The local regression fits are shown by solid lines, the true regression curve by a broken line.

regression function (shown as a broken line) are displayed on each graph. It is clear that the smallest span (0.1) does a poor job of estimating the true regression function because the estimates are much too variable. Likewise, the largest spans (0.7 and 0.9) do a poor job because they have large bias, failing to track the bends in the true regression curve; indeed, the fit for $s = 0.9$ is nearly globally linear. The estimates for intermediate spans (0.3 and 0.5) do a much better job of capturing the true regression. The example takes advantage of our knowledge of the true regression function (knowledge not available, of course, in real applications). Nevertheless, it illustrates how bias and variance change with the span of the local-regression estimator.

To assess the accuracy of the local-regression estimator, we need some way to cumulate mean-squared error over the focal xs at which the estimator is evaluated. One way to do so is to calculate the *average squared error* (ASE),

$$\text{ASE}(s) = \frac{\sum_{i=1}^{n}[\widehat{y}_i(s) - \mu_i]^2}{n},$$

where $\mu_i = E(y \,|\, x_i)$ is the "true" expected value of the response for the ith observation (i.e., using the model in Equation 4.1) and $\widehat{y}_i(s)$ is the ith fitted value for span s. Two points are to be noted here:

1. The squared error is evaluated at the observed x values and then averaged over the n observations.
2. The ASE is calculated for this particular set of data, not as an expectation with respect to repeated sampling.

Figure 4.8 plots the average squared error of the local-linear estimates as a function of span. ASE is minimized for $s \simeq 0.3$, confirming our visual impressions.

4.3.1. Selecting the Span by Cross-Validation

A conceptually appealing, but complex, approach to bandwidth selection is to estimate the optimal h^* formally. We need either to estimate $h^*(x_0)$ for each value x_0 of x at which $\widehat{y} \,|\, x$ is to be evaluated or to estimate an optimal average value to be used with the fixed-bandwidth estimator. A similar approach is applicable to the nearest-neighbor local-regression estimator.

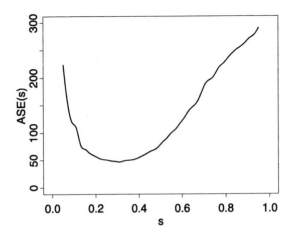

Figure 4.8. Average squared error (ASE) as a function of span (s) for the artificially generated data.

The so-called *plug-in estimate* of h^* proceeds by estimating its components—σ^2, $f''(x_0)$, and $p(x_0)$; we need not estimate the other quantities in Equation 4.3, because the sample size n is known and the constants a_K^2 and s_K^4 can be calculated from the kernel function. Estimating σ^2 and $f''(x_0)$ requires a preliminary estimate of the regression function.

A simpler approach, applicable to both the fixed-bandwidth and the nearest-neighbor estimators, is to estimate the optimal bandwidth or span by *cross-validation*. I consider the nearest-neighbor estimator; the development for the fixed-bandwidth estimator is similar. In cross-validation, we evaluate the regression function at the observations x_i.

The key idea in cross-validation is to *omit* the ith observation from the local regression at the focal value x_i. We denote the resulting estimate of $E(y \mid x_i)$ as $\widehat{y}_{-i} \mid x_i$. Omitting the ith observation makes the fitted value $\widehat{y}_{-i} \mid x_i$ independent of the observed value y_i.

The *cross-validation* (CV) *function* is

$$\mathrm{CV}(s) = \frac{\sum_{i=1}^{n} [\widehat{y}_{-i}(s) - y_i]^2}{n},$$

where $\widehat{y}_{-i}(s)$ is $\widehat{y}_{-i} \mid x_i$ for span s. The object is to find the value of s that minimizes CV. In practice, we need to compute $\mathrm{CV}(s)$ for a range of values of s. Other than repeating the local-regression fit for different values of s, cross-validation does not increase the burden of computation, because we typically evaluate the local regression at each x_i anyway.

The cross-validation function is a kind of estimate of the mean average squared error (MASE) at the observed xs,[7]

$$\text{MASE}(s) = E\left\{ \frac{\sum_{i=1}^{n}[\widehat{y}_i(s) - \mu_i]^2}{n} \right\}.$$

Because of the independence of $\widehat{y}_{-i}$ and y_i, the expectation of $\text{CV}(s)$ is

$$E[\text{CV}(s)] = \frac{\sum_{i=1}^{n} E[\widehat{y}_{-i}(s) - y_i]^2}{n}$$

$$\simeq \text{MASE}(s) + \sigma^2.$$

The substitution of y_i for μ_i increases the expectation of $\text{CV}(s)$ by σ^2, but because σ^2 is a constant, the value of s that minimizes $E[\text{CV}(s)]$ is (approximately) the value that minimizes $\text{MASE}(s)$.

To understand why it is important in this context to omit the ith observation in calculating the fit at the ith observation, consider what would happen were we not to do this. Then, setting the span to 0 would minimize the estimated MASE, because (in the absence of tied x values) the local-regression estimator simply interpolates the observed data: The fitted and observed values are equal, and $\widehat{\text{MASE}}(0) = 0$.

Although cross-validation is often a useful method for selecting the span in local polynomial regression, it should be appreciated that $\text{CV}(s)$ is only an estimate and is, therefore, subject to sampling variation. Particularly in small samples, this variability can be substantial. Moreover, the approximations to the expectation and variance of the local-regression estimator in Equations 4.2 are asymptotic, and, in small samples, $\text{CV}(s)$ often tends to provide values of s that are too small.

Figure 4.9 shows the cross-validation function for the artificial data generated according to Equation 4.1. Compare this graph with Figure 4.8, which shows the actual average square error as a function of span. The error variance $\sigma^2 = 400$ is reflected in the larger values of $\text{CV}(s)$ compared with $\text{ASE}(s)$. In this example, the cross-validation function provides useful guidance in selecting the span.

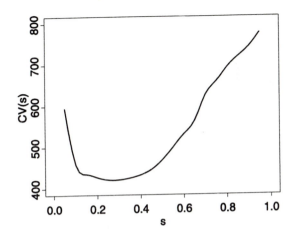

Figure 4.9. The cross-validation function CV(s) for the artificially generated data.

Figure 4.10 shows CV(s) for the regression of occupational prestige on income. In this case, the cross-validation function provides little specific help in selecting the span, suggesting simply that s should be relatively large. Compare this with the value $s \simeq 0.6$ that we arrived at by visual trial and error.

4.4. Making Local Regression Resistant to Outliers

As in linear least squares regression, outliers—and the heavy-tailed error distributions that generate them—can wreak havoc with the local-regression least squares estimator. One solution is to down-weight outlying observations. In linear regression, this strategy leads to *M-estimation*, a kind of robust regression (see, e.g., Fox, 1997, sect. 14.3). The same strategy is applicable to local polynomial regression.

Suppose that we fit a local regression to the data, obtaining estimates $\widehat{y}_i$ and residuals $e_i = y_i - \widehat{y}_i$. Large residuals represent observations that are relatively remote from the fitted regression. Now define weights $W_i = W(e_i)$, where the symmetric function $W(\cdot)$ assigns maximum weight to residuals of 0 and decreasing weight as the absolute residuals grow.

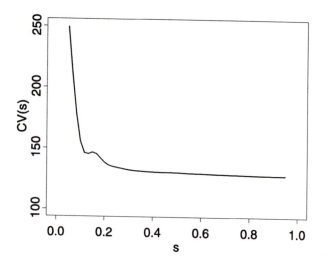

Figure 4.10. Cross-validation function for the local-linear regression of prestige on income.

- One popular choice of weight function is the *bisquare* or *biweight*:

$$W_i = W_B(e_i) = \begin{cases} \left[1 - \left(\dfrac{e_i}{cS} \right)^2 \right]^2 & \text{for } |e_i| < cS, \\ 0 & \text{for } |e_i| \geq cS, \end{cases}$$

where S is a (preferably robust) measure of spread of the residuals, such as the *median absolute residual*, $S = \text{median}|e_i|$, and c is a *tuning constant*, balancing resistance to outliers against efficiency in the event of normal errors. Smaller values of c produce greater resistance to outliers (because observations for which $|e_i| \geq cS$ receive 0 weight), but lower efficiency when the errors are normally distributed. Selecting $c = 7$ (and using the median absolute deviation as a measure of spread) yields about 95% efficiency compared with least squares when the errors are normal; the slightly smaller value $c = 6$ is usually used.

- Another common choice is the *Huber weight function*:

$$W_i = W_H(e_i) = \begin{cases} 1 & \text{for } |e_i| \leq cS, \\ cS/|e_i| & \text{for } |e_i| > cS. \end{cases}$$

Unlike the biweight, the Huber weight function never quite reaches 0. The tuning constant $c = 2$ produces roughly 95% efficiency for normally distributed errors.

The bisquare and Huber weight functions are graphed in Figure 4.11.

Having calculated robustness weights, we refit the local regression at the focal values x_i by WLS, in each case minimizing the weighted residual sum of squares $\sum_{i=1}^{n} w_i^2 W_i^2 e_i^2$, where the W_i are the "robustness" weights just defined and the w_i are the kernel "neighborhood" weights. Finally, because an outlier will influence the initial local fits and, consequently, the residuals and robustness weights, it is necessary to iterate (repeat) this procedure, calculating new residuals from the new fit, calculating new robustness weights from the new residuals, and refitting the local regressions yet again. The entire procedure is repeated until the fitted values $\widehat{y}_i$ stop changing. Two to four robustness iterations almost always suffice.

Recall, from Section 1.1, the United Nations data on infant mortality and GDP per capita for 193 countries. Figure 4.12 shows robust

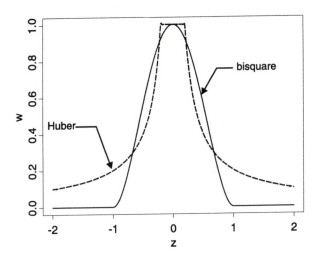

Figure 4.11. The bisquare (solid line) and Huber (broken line) weight functions. The Huber weight function has been rescaled to facilitate the comparison.

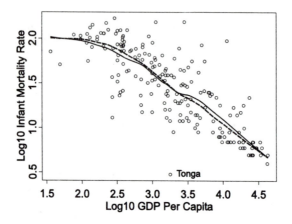

Figure 4.12. Local-linear regressions of log infant-mortality rates on log GDP per capita. The solid line shows the fit without robustness weights. The broken line shows the fit after four robustness iterations. Both fits use the span $s = 0.4$.

and nonrobust local linear regressions of log infant mortality on log GDP. Note how the nonrobust fit is pulled toward relatively extreme observations such as Tonga.

Local regression with nearest-neighbor tricube weights and bisquare robustness weights was introduced by Cleveland (1979), who called the procedure *lowess*, for *lo*cally *w*eighted *s*catterplot *s*moothing. Upon generalizing the method to multiple regression (see the companion to this monograph, Fox, in press), Cleveland, Grosse, and Shyu (1992) rechristened it *loess*, for *lo*cal regre*ss*ion. Lowess (or loess) is the most widely available method of nonparametric regression.

4.4.1. Normal Quantile-Comparison Plots of Residuals

We can use the robust fitting procedure as a matter of course, sacrificing a small amount of efficiency when the errors are really normally distributed, or we can examine the distribution of residuals from a preliminary nonrobust local regression to decide whether a robust fit is required. Examining the residuals is useful in any event for revealing outlying observations. Outliers invite an explanation.

Quantile-comparison plots are particularly useful for comparing data (here, residuals) to a theoretical distribution, such as the normal distribution. Plotting ordered residuals against the corresponding quantiles of the normal distribution helps to detect skewness, heavy-tailed residuals, and outliers. Several alternative univariate displays were described by Jacoby (1997).

Let $e_{(1)}, e_{(2)}, \ldots, e_{(n)}$ represent the ordered residuals and let

$$z_i = \Phi^{-1}\left(\frac{i - \frac{1}{2}}{n}\right), \qquad i = 1, \ldots, n,$$

be the corresponding quantiles of the standard-normal distribution (Φ^{-1} is the inverse of the cumulative normal distribution function). To take a simple example, if $n = 101$ and $i = 51$, then the cumulative proportion of the data below the 51st observation is $(51 - 0.5)/101 = 0.5$; that is, half the residuals are counted at or below $e_{(51)}$. The corresponding normal quantile is $z_{51} = \Phi^{-1}(0.5) = 0$. The normal quantile-comparison plot is formed as a scatterplot of $e_{(i)}$ on the vertical axis against z_i on the horizontal axis.

If the residuals are approximately normally distributed and the average residual is near 0, then $e_{(i)} \simeq Sz_i$, where S is the standard deviation of the residuals. We can judge departures from normality by placing a comparison line on the plot, drawing the line through the point $(0, 0)$ with slope S or more robustly passing a line through the quartiles of e and z. (The quartiles of the standard-normal distribution are at ± 0.674.) In the latter event, we can think of the slope of the line as a robust estimate of σ.

Systematic deviations of the plotted points from the comparison line reveal different kinds of nonnormality:

- A heavy-tailed distribution produces points above the comparison line at the right and below the line at the left.
- Outliers are points that stand out from adjacent points at either end of the distribution—above the other points at the right or below the other points at the left.
- A positively skewed distribution produces points above the line both at the right and the left; a negatively skewed distribution produces points below the line at both ends.

Judging departures from normality is assisted by an indication of sampling variability in the quantile-comparison plot. Suppose that the residuals e_i were drawn independently from a normal distribution with standard deviation S; this is not quite the case—the residuals are somewhat correlated with one another—but we are only looking for a rough approximation. Let $P_i = (i-0.5)/n$ be the cumulative proportion of the data at and below the ith ordered residual, $e_{(i)}$. Then the estimated standard error (SE) of $e_{(i)}$ is

$$\widehat{SE}(e_{(i)}) = \frac{S}{\phi(z_i)}\sqrt{\frac{P_i(1 - P_i)}{n}},$$

where $\phi(z_i)$ is the standard-normal density (the height of the normal curve) at the comparison value z_i. Let $\widehat{e}_{(i)}$ represent the point above z_i on the comparison line. Then

$$\widehat{e}_{(i)} \pm 2\widehat{SE}(e_{(i)})$$

gives an approximate pointwise 95% confidence envelope around the fitted line.

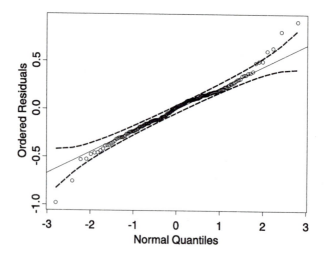

Figure 4.13. Normal quantile-comparison plot of the residuals from the local-linear regression of log infant mortality on log GDP per capita. The comparison line is drawn through the quartiles; the broken lines give an approximate pointwise 95% confidence interval around the fitted line.

Figure 4.13 shows a normal quantile-comparison plot of residuals from the nonrobust local-linear regression of log infant mortality on log GDP per capita. The points on the plot pull away from the comparison line in a pattern characteristic of a heavy-tailed distribution, suggesting the desirability of a robust fit to the data.

4.5. Displaying Spread and Asymmetry*

The foregoing discussion assumes implicitly—and sometimes explicitly—that the conditional variation of y is constant $[V(y \mid x) = V(\varepsilon) = \sigma^2]$ and that the conditional distribution of y is symmetric around its mean, $\mu \mid x$. If the spread of y is not constant, then it would be useful to discover how it changes as a function of x. If the distribution of $y \mid x$ is not symmetric, then it is not reasonable to summarize the center of this distribution with the conditional mean.

Suppose now that the conditional variance $V(y \mid x_0) = \sigma^2 \mid x_0$ changes as the focal value x_0 changes. The conditional variance is a kind of mean (i.e., an expectation):

$$\sigma^2 \mid x_0 = E\big[(y \mid x_0 - \mu \mid x_0)^2\big].$$

We already know how to estimate $\mu \mid x_0$ by the fitted value $\widehat{y} \mid x_0$ from the local polynomial regression of y on x. Consequently, ignoring any bias in the local-regression estimate, the average squared residual at x_0—that is, mean$[(y \mid x_0 - \widehat{y} \mid x_0)^2]$—estimates $\sigma^2 \mid x_0$.

We could apply this result directly if there were many replicated observations at each focal value x_0 of x. That this is generally not the case motivated the kernel and local polynomial estimators: Considering all observations in a neighborhood near the focal value x_0 allowed us to assemble enough data to estimate $\mu \mid x_0$, smoothing y against x.

In the absence of replicated observations at x_0, we can similarly smooth the squared residuals from the local polynomial fit to estimate the conditional (i.e., local) error variance $\sigma^2 \mid x_0$. In this context, I prefer the kernel estimator to the local polynomial estimator, because locally weighted averages of squared residuals cannot be negative, whereas local polynomial estimates can. A negative variance, of course, is uninterpretable. If there are outliers or if the residual distribution is heavy-tailed, then we can compute a robust measure of spread by using robustness weights.

When the conditional distribution of y at x_0 is symmetric, separate estimates of $\sigma^2 \mid x_0$ based on negative and positive residuals should be roughly equal. If, alternatively, this distribution is positively skewed, then the estimate of $\sigma^2 \mid x_0$ based on negative residuals should be smaller than that based on positive residuals. A negative skew produces the opposite pattern. We can, therefore, check for skewness by forming two sets of estimates of $\sigma^2 \mid x_0$, separately smoothing squared positive and negative residuals against x (see the subsequent example).

Figure 4.14 illustrates the application of these ideas to the Canadian occupational prestige data. Figure 4.14(a) shows the local linear regression of prestige against income (the solid line), along with an estimated one-standard-deviation band around the fit, $\hat{y} \mid x \pm \hat{\sigma} \mid x$ (the broken lines). The conditional standard deviation $\hat{\sigma} \mid x$ was obtained from the square root of the kernel regression of squared residuals on prestige, as described previously. In Figure 4.14(b), the conditional standard deviation is estimated separately from negative $\hat{\sigma}_- \mid x$ and positive $\hat{\sigma}_+ \mid x$ residuals, and the band is defined by $\hat{y} \mid x - \hat{\sigma}_- \mid x$ and $\hat{y} \mid x + \hat{\sigma}_+ \mid x$. There is little evidence of nonconstant spread in either graph, but there is some suggestion of slight positive skew in Figure 4.14(b), because, through much of the range of x, the fitted regression function $\hat{y} \mid x$ is somewhat closer to the lower curve, $\hat{y} \mid x - \hat{\sigma}_- \mid x$, than to the upper one, $\hat{y} \mid x + \hat{\sigma}_+ \mid x$.

4.6. Smoothing Time-Series Data*

A common application of scatterplot smoothing is to time-series data, where the predictor variable is time and observations are evenly spaced. Here we implicitly use the model

$$y_t = f(t) + \varepsilon_t$$

for times $t = 1, 2, \ldots, n$. The regression function $f(t)$ represents the *trend* of the response variable y, and the errors ε_t represent departures from the trend. Because the errors ε_t are ordered in time, it is generally unreasonable to assume that they are independent.

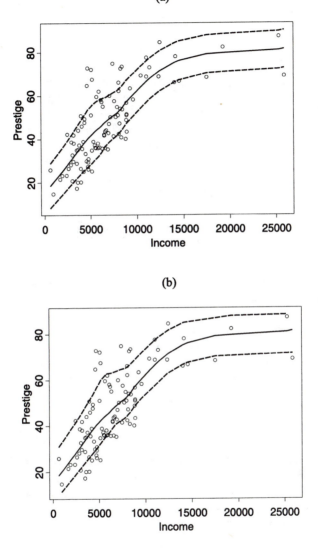

Figure 4.14. Local-linear regression of occupational prestige on income (solid line) showing ±1 standard deviation from the fit (broken lines). In (a), the standard deviation is obtained by kernel smoothing of squared residuals against income. In (b), squared positive and negative residuals are smoothed separately. In all cases, the span of the smoothers is $s = 0.6$.

For simplicity and concreteness, suppose that the errors follow a *first-order autoregressive process*,

$$\varepsilon_t = \rho \varepsilon_{t-1} + v_t,$$

where ε_{t-1} is the error for the previous time point, $|\rho| < 1$, and the v_t are independent "disturbances" with zero means and constant variance. Then ρ is the *autocorrelation* between ε_t and ε_{t-1}. The results that I am about to describe also hold qualitatively for other, more complex error-generating processes.

Recall from Section 4.3 that when the errors are independent, the optimal bandwidth for the local-linear smoother at focal value x_0 is (repeating Equation 4.3)

$$h^*(x_0) = \left[\frac{a_K^2}{s_K^4} \times \frac{\sigma^2}{np(x_0)\left[f''(x_0)\right]^2} \right]^{1/5},$$

where the constants a_K^2 and s_K^4 are properties of the kernel function. A small error variance (σ^2), a large n, a dense region of data [large $p(x_0)$], and a rough regression function [large $f''(x_0)$] are all factors that favor a small bandwidth. For time-series data, the data density $p(t)$ is constant, but the other factors behave similarly.

When the errors follow a first-order autoregressive process, the optimal bandwidth at focal time point t_0 is[8]

$$h^*(t_0; \rho) = \left(\frac{2}{1-\rho} - 1 \right)^{1/5} h^*(t_0).$$

Positively autocorrelated errors ($\rho > 0$), therefore, require a larger bandwidth than otherwise similar data with uncorrelated errors (and negatively autocorrelated errors require a smaller bandwidth). This result is intuitively reasonable, since positive autocorrelation in the errors is a source of cyclical smoothness in the data that could be mistaken for the trend $f(t)$.

All this presupposes knowledge of the error autocorrelation ρ. If we do not know ρ, as is universally the case in applications, then we need to estimate it from the data. In parametric time-series regression, where we start with knowledge of the form of $f(t)$ up to unknown parameters (or *pretend* that we have this knowledge), we can fit a preliminary model to the data and estimate ρ from the residuals. In nonparametric regression (e.g., Fox, 1997, sect. 14.1; Ostrom, 1990), however, ρ is underidentified (i.e., indeterminate), because the autocorrelation of the residuals depends crucially on the bandwidth of a preliminary nonparametric-regression estimate, and the estimated "optimal" span depends crucially on the estimate of ρ.

Put another way, without knowledge of ρ or some other equivalently relevant prior information, we cannot distinguish smoothness in the data due to trend in the regression function $f(t)$ from smoothness due to autocorrelation ρ of the errors. Moreover, inasmuch as the model $y_t = f(t) + \varepsilon_t$ is typically meant simply as a description of the data, there is no good way to resolve this ambiguity. Choosing the smoothing parameter to provide a good visual fit to the data is as justified as more complex approaches (see, e.g., Bowman & Azzalini, 1997, chap. 7) that try to make plausible assumptions about the trade-off of trend against autocorrelation.

Figure 4.15 shows the annual homicide rate per million inhabitants for Metropolitan Toronto in the period 1960 through 1996. Nearest-neighbor local-quadratic fits to the data are given for several spans[9]: The fit for span = 0.2 in panel (a) nearly interpolates the data; the fit for span = 0.6 in panel (b) seems a more reasonable balance of smoothness against detail; the fit for span = 1.0 in panel (c) appears oversmooth; and the global quadratic least squares fit in panel (d), corresponding to an infinite span, misrepresents the trend in the data. (The presence of an obviously outlying year—1991—suggests the possibility of using a robust fit. Note, as well, that a local-polynomial regression is not well suited to capturing the apparent jump in the homicide rate around 1971.)

Figure 4.16 graphs the residual autocorrelation

$$\widehat{\rho} = \frac{\sum_{i=2}^{n} e_t e_{t-1}}{\sum_{i=1}^{n} e_t^2}$$

as a function of span, illustrating how the autocorrelation depends crucially on the span. For small spans, the residual autocorrelation is large and negative; it is nearer zero for intermediate spans and small but positive for larger spans. For the global quadratic least squares fit (not shown in Figure 4.16), $\widehat{\rho} = 0.273$.

50

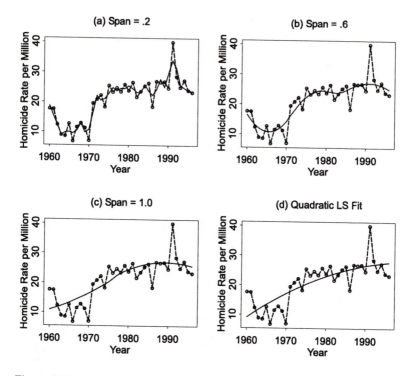

Figure 4.15. The solid lines show various local-quadratic fits to the Toronto homicide-rate data: (a) span = 0.2; (b) span = 0.6; (c) span = 1.0; (d) global quadratic least squares fit (i.e., infinite span).

5. STATISTICAL INFERENCE FOR LOCAL-POLYNOMIAL REGRESSION

In parametric regression—for example, linear least squares regression—the central objects of estimation are the regression coefficients. Statistical inference naturally focuses on these coefficients, typically taking the form of confidence intervals or hypothesis tests. In nonparametric regression, in contrast, there are no regression coefficients. Instead, the central object of estimation is the regression function, and inference focuses on the regression function directly.

Many applications of nonparametric regression with one predictor simply have as their goal visual smoothing of a scatterplot. In these instances, statistical inference is, at best, of secondary interest. Infer-

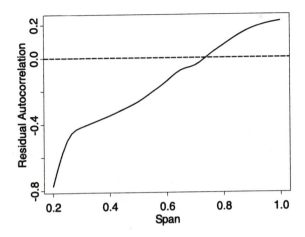

Figure 4.16. Residual autocorrelation as a function of span, for local-quadratic fits to the Toronto homicide-rate data.

ence becomes more prominent in nonparametric multiple regression (addressed in the companion monograph, Fox, in press).

This section takes up several aspects of statistical inference for local-polynomial regression with one predictor. I start by explaining how to construct an approximate confidence envelope for the regression function. Then I present a simple approach to hypothesis testing, based on an analogy to procedures for testing hypotheses in linear least squares regression. The statistical theory behind these relatively simple methods is subsequently examined, and some alternatives, including empirical resampling from the data, are briefly developed.

5.1. Confidence Envelopes

Consider the local polynomial estimate $\widehat{f}(x) = \widehat{y} \,|\, x$ of the regression function $f(x)$. For notational convenience, I assume that the regression function is evaluated at the observed predictor values, $x_1, x_2, \ldots, x_n$, although the line of reasoning to be developed here is more general.

The fitted value $\widehat{y}_i = \widehat{y} \,|\, x_i$ results from a locally weighted least squares regression of y on the x values. This fitted value is therefore a weighted sum of the observations (see Section 5.3 for this and other results),

$$\widehat{y}_i = \sum_{j=1}^{n} s_{ij} y_j,$$

where the weights s_{ij} are functions of the x values. (The situation is more complex when there are robustness iterations, because then the weights also depend on the y values.) For the tricube weight function, for example, s_{ij} is 0 for any observations outside of the neighborhood of the focal x_i. Because (by assumption) the y_is are independently distributed, with common conditional variance $V(y \mid x = x_i) = V(y_i) = \sigma^2$, the sampling variance of the fitted value $\widehat{y}_i$ is

$$V(\widehat{y}_i) = \sigma^2 \sum_{j=1}^{n} s_{ij}^2.$$

To apply this result, we require an estimate of σ^2. In linear least squares simple regression, we estimate the error variance as

$$S^2 = \frac{\sum e_i^2}{n-2},$$

where $e_i = y_i - \widehat{y}_i$ is the residual for observation i, and $n-2$ is the degrees of freedom associated with the residual sum of squares. We "lose" 2 degrees of freedom as a consequence of estimating the two regression parameters—the intercept α and the slope β.

We can calculate residuals in nonparametric regression in the same manner—that is, $e_i = y_i - \widehat{y}_i$, where, of course, that fitted value $\widehat{y}_i$ is from the nonparametric regression. To complete the analogy, we require the *equivalent number of parameters* or *equivalent degrees of freedom* for the model, df_{mod} (as described in Section 5.3), from which we can obtain the residual degrees of freedom, $df_{\text{res}} = n - df_{\text{mod}}$. Then, the estimated error variance is

$$S^2 = \frac{\sum e_i^2}{df_{\text{res}}}$$

and the estimated variance of the fitted value $\widehat{y}_i$ at $x = x_i$ is

$$\widehat{V}(\widehat{y}_i) = S^2 \sum_{j=1}^{n} s_{ij}^2. \tag{5.1}$$

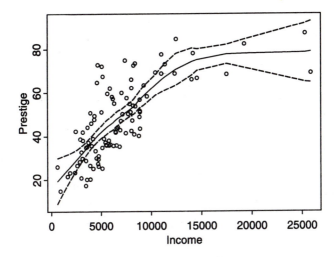

Figure 5.1. Local-linear regression of occupational prestige on income, showing an approximate pointwise 95% confidence envelope. The span of the smoother is $s = 0.6$.

Assuming normally distributed errors or a sufficiently large sample, a 95% confidence interval for $E(y \mid x_i) = f(x_i)$ is approximately

$$\widehat{y}_i \pm 2\sqrt{\widehat{V}(\widehat{y}_i)}. \tag{5.2}$$

Putting the confidence intervals together for $x = x_1, x_2, \ldots, x_n$ produces a *pointwise 95% confidence band* or *confidence envelope* for the regression function. In a pointwise confidence band, the confidence statement applies separately at each x_i. Constructing a *simultaneous* confidence band for the regression function as a whole is a much more difficult—and less practical—endeavor.

An example, employing the local-linear regression of prestige on income in the Canadian occupational prestige data (with span $s = 0.6$), appears in Figure 5.1. Here, $df_{\mathrm{mod}} = 5.0$ and $S^2 = 12{,}004.72/(102 - 5.0) = 123.76$. The nonparametric-regression curve therefore uses the equivalent of five parameters—roughly the same as a fourth-degree polynomial. The following two points should be noted:

1. Although the locally linear fit uses the *equivalent* of five parameters, it does not produce the same regression curve as fitting a global fourth-degree polynomial to the data.
2. In this instance, the equivalent number of parameters rounds to an integer, but this is an accident of the example and is not generally the case.

Although this procedure for constructing a confidence band has the virtue of simplicity, it is not quite correct, due to the bias in $\widehat{y}\,|\,x$ as an estimate of $E(y\,|\,x)$. If we have chosen the span and degree of the local-polynomial estimator judiciously, however, the bias should be small. Bias in $\widehat{y}\,|\,x$ has the following consequences:

- S^2 is biased upward, tending to overstate the error variance and making the confidence interval too wide. Bowman and Azzalini (1997, sect. 4.3) considered alternative approaches to estimating the error variance σ^2.
- The confidence interval is, on average, centered in the wrong location.

These errors tend to offset each other. Because $\widehat{y}\,|\,x$ is biased, it is more accurate to describe the envelope around the sample regression constructed from Equation 5.2 as a *"variability band"* rather than as a confidence band.

5.2. Hypothesis Tests

In linear least squares regression, F tests of hypotheses are formulated by comparing alternative nested models. To say that two models are nested means that one, the more specific model, is a special case of the other, more general model. For example, in least squares linear simple regression, the F statistic

$$F = \frac{\text{TSS} - \text{RSS}}{\text{RSS}/(n-2)}$$

with 1 and $n-2$ degrees of freedom tests the hypothesis of no linear relationship between y and x. Here, the total sum of squares, TSS $= \sum(y_i - \overline{y})^2$, is the variation in y associated with the null model of no relationship, $y_i = \alpha + \varepsilon_i$, and the residual sum of squares, RSS $=$

$\sum (y_i - \hat{y}_i)^2$, represents the variation in y conditional on the linear relationship between y and x, based on residuals from the model $y_i = \alpha + \beta x_i + \varepsilon_i$. Because the null model is a special case of the linear model, with $\beta = 0$, the two models are nested.

An analogous, but more general, F test of no relationship for the nonparametric-regression model is

$$F = \frac{(\text{TSS} - \text{RSS})/(df_{\text{mod}} - 1)}{\text{RSS}/df_{\text{res}}} \qquad (5.3)$$

with $df_{\text{mod}} - 1$ and $df_{\text{res}} = n - df_{\text{mod}}$ degrees of freedom. Here RSS is the residual sum of squares for the nonparametric-regression model. Applied to the local-linear regression of prestige on income, where $n = 102$, TSS $= 29,895.43$, RSS $= 12,004.72$, and $df_{\text{mod}} = 5.0$, we have

$$F = \frac{(29,895.43 - 12,004.72)/(5.0 - 1)}{12,004.72/(102 - 5.0)} = 36.14$$

with $5.0 - 1 = 4.0$ and $102 - 5.0 = 97.0$ degrees of freedom. The resulting p value is much smaller than 0.0001, casting substantial doubt on the null hypothesis of no relationship between prestige and income of occupations.

A test of nonlinearity is simply constructed by contrasting the nonparametric-regression model with the linear simple-regression model. The models are properly nested because a linear relationship is a special case of a general, potentially nonlinear, relationship. Denoting the residual sum of squares from the linear model as RSS_0 and the residual sum of squares from the more general nonparametric-regression model as RSS_1, we have

$$F = \frac{(\text{RSS}_0 - \text{RSS}_1)/(df_{\text{mod}} - 2)}{\text{RSS}_1/df_{\text{res}}}$$

with $df_{\text{mod}} - 2$ and $df_{\text{res}} = n - df_{\text{mod}}$ degrees of freedom. This test is constructed according to the rule that the most general model—here the nonparametric-regression model—is employed for estimating the error variance, $S^2 = \text{RSS}_1/df_{\text{res}}$. For the regression of occupational prestige on income, $\text{RSS}_0 = 14,616.17$, $\text{RSS}_1 = 12,004.72$, and

$df_{\text{mod}} = 5.0$; thus

$$F = \frac{(14{,}616.17 - 12{,}004.72)/(5.0 - 2)}{12{,}004.72/(102 - 5.0)} = 7.03$$

with $5.0 - 2 = 3.0$ and $102 - 5.0 = 97.0$ degrees of freedom. The corresponding p value, 0.0003, suggests that the relationship between the two variables is significantly nonlinear.

5.3. Some Statistical Details and Alternative Inference Procedures*

5.3.1. The Smoother Matrix and the Variance of $\widehat{y}$

As noted in Section 5.1, the fitted values $\widehat{y}_i$ in local-polynomial regression are weighted sums of the observed y values:

$$\widehat{y}_i = \sum_{j=1}^{n} s_{ij} y_j.$$

Let us collect the weights s_{ij} into the *smoother matrix*

$$\mathbf{S}_{(n \times n)} = \begin{bmatrix} s_{11} & s_{12} & \cdots & s_{1i} & \cdots & s_{1n} \\ s_{21} & s_{22} & \cdots & s_{2i} & \cdots & s_{2n} \\ \vdots & \vdots & \ddots & \vdots & & \vdots \\ s_{i1} & s_{i2} & \cdots & s_{ii} & \cdots & s_{in} \\ \vdots & \vdots & & \vdots & \ddots & \vdots \\ s_{n1} & s_{n2} & \cdots & s_{ni} & \cdots & s_{nn} \end{bmatrix}$$

Then

$$\widehat{\mathbf{y}}_{(n \times 1)} = \mathbf{S} \mathbf{y}_{(n \times 1)},$$

where $\widehat{\mathbf{y}} = [\widehat{y}_1, \widehat{y}_2, \ldots, \widehat{y}_n]'$ is the column vector of fitted values and $\mathbf{y} = [y_1, y_2, \ldots, y_n]'$ is the column vector of observed response values. The covariance matrix of the fitted values is

$$V(\widehat{\mathbf{y}}) = \mathbf{S} V(\mathbf{y}) \mathbf{S}' = \sigma^2 \mathbf{S} \mathbf{S}'. \tag{5.4}$$

This result follows from the assumptions that the conditional variance of y_i is constant (σ^2) and that the observations are independent, implying that $V(\mathbf{y}) = \sigma^2 \mathbf{I}_n$ (where $\mathbf{I}_n$ is the order-n identity matrix). Equation 5.1 for the variance of $\widehat{y}_i$ is just an expansion of the ith diagonal entry of $V(\widehat{\mathbf{y}})$.

Recall that the *linear*-regression model is written $\mathbf{y} = \mathbf{X}\boldsymbol{\beta} + \boldsymbol{\varepsilon}$, where $\mathbf{X}$ is the model matrix of predictors, $\boldsymbol{\beta}$ is the vector of regression parameters to be estimated, and $\boldsymbol{\varepsilon}$ is the error vector. The smoother matrix $\mathbf{S}$ in nonparametric regression plays a key role in developing the statistical properties of the local-regression estimator. It is analogous to the *hat matrix* $\mathbf{H} = \mathbf{X}(\mathbf{X}'\mathbf{X})^{-1}\mathbf{X}'$ in linear least squares regression, so named because $\mathbf{H}$ projects the observed values into the predictor space to obtain the fitted values, $\widehat{\mathbf{y}} = \mathbf{H}\mathbf{y}$, thus putting the "hat" on $\mathbf{y}$ (see, e.g., Fox, 1991). The residuals in linear least squares regression are

$$\mathbf{e} = \mathbf{y} - \widehat{\mathbf{y}} = (\mathbf{I}_n - \mathbf{H})y.$$

The analogous expression in local regression is

$$\mathbf{e} = \mathbf{y} - \widehat{\mathbf{y}} = (\mathbf{I}_n - \mathbf{S})\mathbf{y}.$$

To determine the smoother matrix $\mathbf{S}$, recall that $\widehat{y}_i$ results from a locally weighted polynomial regression of y on x,

$$y_j = a_i + b_{1i}(x_j - x_i) + b_{2i}(x_j - x_i)^2 + \cdots + b_{pi}(x_j - x_i)^p + e_{ji},$$

where the weights $w_{ji} = K[(x_j - x_i)/h]$ decline with distance from the focal x_i. The local-regression coefficients are chosen to minimize $\sum_{j=1}^{n} w_{ji}^2 e_{ji}^2$. The fitted value $\widehat{y}_i$ is just the regression constant a_i. In matrix form, the local regression is

$$\mathbf{y} = \mathbf{X}_i \mathbf{b}_i + \mathbf{e}_i.$$

The model matrix $\mathbf{X}_i$ contains the predictors in the local-regression equation (including an initial column of 1s for the constant), and the coefficient vector $\mathbf{b}_i$ contains the regression coefficients.

Define the diagonal matrix $\mathbf{W}_i = \text{diag}\{w_{ji}\}$ of kernel weights. Then the local-regression coefficients are

$$\mathbf{b}_i = (\mathbf{X}_i'\mathbf{W}_i\mathbf{X}_i)^{-1}\mathbf{X}_i'\mathbf{W}_i\mathbf{y}$$

and the ith row of the smoother matrix is the first row of $(\mathbf{X}_i'\mathbf{W}_i\mathbf{X}_i)^{-1}\mathbf{X}_i'\mathbf{W}_i$ (i.e., the row that determines the constant, $a_i = \widehat{y}_i$). To construct $\mathbf{S}$ we need to repeat this procedure for $i = 1, 2, \ldots, n$.

5.3.2. Degrees of Freedom

In linear least squares regression, the degrees of freedom for the model can be defined in a variety of equivalent ways. Most directly, assuming that the model matrix $\mathbf{X}$ is of full column rank, the degrees of freedom for the model are equal to the number of predictors k (including the regression intercept). The degrees of freedom for the model are also equal to

- the rank and trace (i.e., sum of diagonal elements) of the projection matrix, $\mathbf{H}$;
- the trace of $\mathbf{HH}'$;
- the trace of $2\mathbf{H} - \mathbf{HH}'$.

These alternative expressions follow from the fact that the hat matrix is symmetric and idempotent—that is, $\mathbf{H} = \mathbf{H}'$ and $\mathbf{H} = \mathbf{HH}$. The degrees of freedom for error in least-squares linear regression are

$$df_{\text{res}} = \text{rank}(\mathbf{I}_n - \mathbf{H}) = \text{trace}(\mathbf{I}_n - \mathbf{H}) = n - \text{trace}(\mathbf{H})$$

because $\mathbf{I}_n - \mathbf{H}$ projects $\mathbf{y}$ onto the orthogonal complement of the column space of $\mathbf{X}$ to obtain the residuals: $\mathbf{e} = (\mathbf{I}_n - \mathbf{H})\mathbf{y}$.

Analogous degrees of freedom for the local-regression model are obtained by substituting the smoother matrix $\mathbf{S}$ for the hat matrix $\mathbf{H}$. The analogy is not perfect, however, and, in general, $\text{trace}(\mathbf{S}) \neq \text{trace}(\mathbf{SS}') \neq \text{trace}(2\mathbf{S} - \mathbf{SS}')$.

- Defining $df_{\text{mod}} = \text{trace}(\mathbf{S})$ is an attractive choice because it is easy to calculate.
- In a linear model, the degrees of freedom for the model are equal to the sum of variances of the fitted values divided by the error variance,

$$\frac{\sum_{i=1}^{n} V(\widehat{y}_i)}{\sigma^2} = k.$$

In the current context (from Equation 5.4),

$$\frac{\sum_{i=1}^{n} V(\widehat{y}_i)}{\sigma^2} = \text{trace}(\mathbf{SS}'),$$

motivating the definition, $df_{\text{mod}} = \text{trace}(\mathbf{SS}')$.

- The expectation of the residual sum of squares in local-polynomial regression is (Hastie & Tibshirani, 1990, sect. 3.4 and 3.5)

$$E(\text{RSS}) = \sigma^2 \left[n - \text{trace}(2\mathbf{S} - \mathbf{SS}') \right] + \text{bias}^2,$$

where $\text{bias}^2 = \sum_{i=1}^{n} [E(\hat{y}_i) - f(x_i)]^2$ is the cumulative bias in the local regression evaluated at the observed x values. If the bias is negligible, then $\text{RSS}/[n - \text{trace}(2\mathbf{S} - \mathbf{SS}')]$ is an estimator of the error variance σ^2, suggesting that $n - \text{trace}(2\mathbf{S} - \mathbf{SS}')$ is a suitable definition of the degrees of freedom for error and that $df_{\text{mod}} = \text{trace}(2\mathbf{S} - \mathbf{SS}')$. This last definition is possibly the most attractive theoretically, but it is relatively difficult to compute. Hastie and Tibshirani (1990, sect. 3.5) demonstrated a simple relationship between $\text{trace}(2\mathbf{S} - \mathbf{SS}')$ and $\text{trace}(\mathbf{S})$ that allows the latter to be used to approximate the former. The software used to generate the examples in the current text takes this approach.[10]

Further discussion of these issues may be found in Hastie and Tibshirani (1990, sect. 3.5) and in Cleveland, Grosse, and Shyu (1992, sect. 8.4.1). Hastie and Tibshirani (1990, sect. 3.8 and 3.9) showed how incremental F tests can be made more precise by adjusting the degrees of freedom used in finding p values. Similar procedures can be applied to improve the performance of confidence bands for the regression curve, using the t distribution in the calculation of margins of error.

5.3.3. A Caveat

The approach to inference described in this section depends on an analogy between nonparametric smoothing and linear least squares regression. This approach appears to work well in practice, but, as far as I am aware, it has no deep justification. A more complex alternative is to derive the approximate distribution of a test statistic for a hypothesis under the assumption of normally distributed errors. The presentation here follows Bowman and Azzalini (1997, chap. 5).

Consider, for example, the general test of no relationship described in Section 5.2. Here we contrast two models: a more general nonparametric-regression model, with residual sum of squares

$$\text{RSS}_1 = \mathbf{y}'(\mathbf{I}_n - \mathbf{S})'(\mathbf{I}_n - \mathbf{S})\mathbf{y} = \mathbf{y}'\mathbf{A}\mathbf{y},$$

and the more specific null model, with residual sum of squares

$$\text{RSS}_0 = \mathbf{y}'(\mathbf{I}_n - \mathbf{H}_0)'(\mathbf{I}_n - \mathbf{H}_0)\mathbf{y} = \mathbf{y}'(\mathbf{I}_n - \mathbf{H}_0)\mathbf{y}.$$

In the null model, the fitted value for each observation is simply $\bar{y}$, so the corresponding hat matrix is $\mathbf{H}_0 = \{1/n\}_{(n \times n)}$. The sum of squares to test the null hypothesis is then

$$\text{RSS}_0 - \text{RSS}_1 = \mathbf{y}'[\mathbf{I}_n - \mathbf{H}_0 - (\mathbf{I}_n - \mathbf{S})'(\mathbf{I_n} - \mathbf{S})]\mathbf{y} = \mathbf{y}'\mathbf{By}.$$

Form the test statistic

$$T = \frac{\text{RSS}_0 - \text{RSS}_1}{\text{RSS}_0} = \frac{\mathbf{y}'\mathbf{By}}{\mathbf{y}'\mathbf{Ay}}. \tag{5.5}$$

Notice that here RSS_0 is just the total sum of squares for y, so the test statistic T is the R^2 for the nonparametric regression; this is only the case for the null hypothesis of no relationship. Assuming the truth of the hypothesis and letting T^* represent the obtained value of the test statistic, the p value for the test is

$$p = \Pr\left(\frac{\mathbf{y}'\mathbf{By}}{\mathbf{y}'\mathbf{Ay}} > T^*\right) = \Pr[\mathbf{y}'(\mathbf{B} - T^*\mathbf{A})\mathbf{y} > 0].$$

This probability entails a quadratic form in the symmetric matrix $\mathbf{B} - T^*\mathbf{A}$, a case that is well understood when $\mathbf{y}$ is normally distributed. Bowman and Azzalini (1997, chap. 5) described how p can be calculated or approximated. Except for the omission of degrees of freedom, T is the F statistic for testing no relationship given in Equation 5.3.

5.3.4. Bootstrap Confidence Bands

Bootstrapping provides a general approach to statistical inference based on randomly resampling from the observed data. Bootstrapping is an attractive methodology because it does not require strong distributional assumptions and because it is adaptable to contexts in which analytic results are hard to come by. Because its implementation typically substitutes brute-force computation for theoretical derivations, however, a disadvantage of bootstrapping is that it is computationally intensive and may require custom programming.

To implement the bootstrap, we treat the sample as if it were a population, randomly selecting n observations from the data *with replacement* and obtaining estimates for the resulting *bootstrap sample*. We repeat this procedure many times, calculating estimates for each bootstrap replication. Sampling with replacement is necessary here, because otherwise we would simply reproduce the original sample. A consequence of sampling with replacement is that some observations typically appear more than once in the bootstrap sample and others do not appear at all.

The central bootstrap analogy is that *the bootstrap samples are to the original sample as the original sample is to the population.* Thus, by studying how the bootstrap estimates behave when we sample repeatedly, we hope to learn about the sampling distribution of the estimator that we employed in the original sample.

This description assumes that the data are an independent random sample from the population. If some other sampling scheme has been employed, then it should be reflected in the selection of bootstrap samples. The key requirement is to make the selection of bootstrap samples from the sample parallel the selection of the sample from the population—a corollary to the central bootstrap analogy.

For regression data, the bootstrap resamples x, y pairs,

$$\{x_1^*, y_1^*\}, \{x_2^*, y_2^*\}, \ldots, \{x_n^*, y_n^*\},$$

where the asterisks remind us that, for example, $\{x_1^*, y_1^*\}$ is not generally the first observation in the original sample, just the first random draw. We proceed to fit a nonparametric regression to the bootstrap sample, obtaining fitted values at some preset x values, such as the original x_i: $\widehat{y}^* \mid x_1, \widehat{y}^* \mid x_2, \ldots, \widehat{y}^* \mid x_n$. For compactness, write $\widehat{y}^* \mid x_i$ as $\widehat{y}_i^*$.

Now repeat the entire procedure B times, each time selecting a bootstrap sample and recalculating the nonparametric regression. The bth such sample produces fitted values $\widehat{y}_{b1}^*, \widehat{y}_{b2}^*, \ldots, \widehat{y}_{bn}^*$. To construct confidence intervals, B should be quite large—say 1,000 or 2,000.

Figure 5.2 shows 50 bootstrap replications of the local-linear fit for the regression of occupational prestige on income. The variability of the bootstrap regressions gives a sense of sampling variation in the local-regression procedure.

This procedure implicitly treats the x values as random rather than fixed. The bootstrap can also be adapted to fixed-x resampling. Even when x is thought of as fixed (as in an experiment), there are still some advantages to resampling pairs. See, for example, Efron and Tibshirani (1993, sect. 9.5) and Stine (1990) for further discussion of bootstrap resampling in regression with fixed versus random xs.

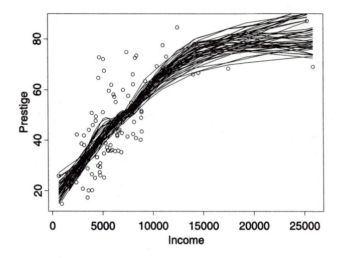

Figure 5.2. Fifty bootstrap replications of the local-linear regression of occupational prestige on income, for span $s = 0.6$.

A simple approach to obtaining a confidence interval for $E(y \mid x_i)$, the regression curve at x_i, is as follows: Focus on the B bootstrap replicates of $\widehat{y}_i^*$, ordering these values from smallest to largest, $\widehat{y}_{(1)i}^*, \widehat{y}_{(2)i}^*, \ldots, \widehat{y}_{(B)i}^*$. Suppose, for simplicity, that we want a 95% confidence interval and that $B = 1{,}000$. Then the endpoints of the *percentile confidence interval* for $E(y \mid x_i)$ are $\widehat{y}_{(25)i}^*$ and $\widehat{y}_{(975)i}^*$, which mark off the 2.5 and 97.5 percentiles of the distribution of $\widehat{y}_i^*$. We need to repeat this calculation at each point at which the regression is evaluated, assembling the results into a pointwise 95% confidence envelope for the nonparametric regression.

Figure 5.3 shows a 95% bootstrap confidence band for the regression of occupational prestige on income based on $B = 2000$ bootstrap replications. This bootstrap confidence band is generally similar to the standard 95% confidence band given previously in Figure 5.1.[11]

The percentile interval does not take into account of the bias of the local-regression estimator. Other, more complicated forms of the bootstrap, can adjust for bias. More extensive discussions of bootstrapping may be found in many sources, including Efron and Tibshirani (1993), Fox (1997, sect. 16.1), Mooney and Duval (1993), and Stine (1990).

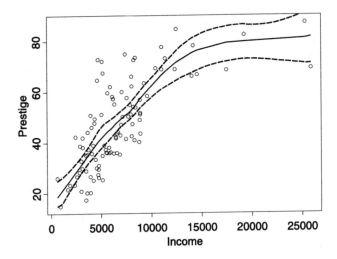

Figure 5.3. The 95% bootstrap percentile confidence envelope for the local-linear regression of occupational prestige on income. The span for the smoother is $s = 0.6$, and the number of bootstrap replications is $B = 2000$.

5.3.5. Randomization Tests

Randomization tests are an empirical inference procedure, similar in spirit to the bootstrap. Randomization tests are applicable to certain kinds of hypotheses in nonparametric regression, such as the null hypothesis of no relationship between y and x. If this hypothesis is correct, then the conditional average value of y given x—that is, $E(y \mid x)$—is everywhere the same. This is true, for example, if the conditional distribution of y given x does not change as x changes, making pairings of x and y values $\{x_i, y_i\}$ essentially arbitrary.

Pursuing this insight, suppose that we calculate a test statistic, such as the T value for the null hypothesis (Equation 5.5 in Section 5.3.3), that assesses the degree of departure of the data from H_0. Call the observed value of this test statistic T^*.[12] Let us then permute the data—arbitrarily pairing x and y values—to obtain a new data set $\{x_i, y_i^*\}$. We proceed to fit the nonparametric regression to the permuted data, calculating the value of the test statistic.

If n is very small, then we can construct all $M = n!$ permutations of the data, recalculating the regression and the test statistic for each one. The distribution of T across the permuted data sets is the empirical sampling distribution of the test statistic assuming the truth of the null hypothesis. The p value for the permutation test is, therefore, the proportion of test statistics in the empirical sampling distribution of T that exceed the observed value T^*,

$$p = \frac{\#_{r=1}^{M}(T_r > T^*)}{M} \qquad (5.6)$$

(where the # operator counts the number of times that the inequality holds).

Unless n is very small, it is impractical to enumerate all of the permuted pairings of x and y values. An effective alternative is to sample a relatively large number of permutations and to calculate an estimate of the permutation-test p value. This procedure is called a randomization test.[13]

Figure 5.4 shows the randomization sampling distribution of the T-test statistic for the null hypothesis of no relationship between prestige

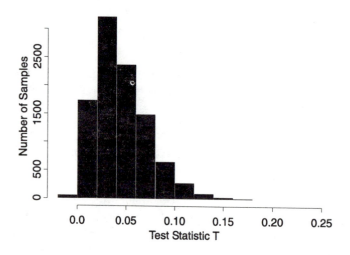

Figure 5.4. Randomization distribution of the T-test statistic for the null hypothesis of no relationship between occupational prestige and income, based on 10,000 permutations of the data and a local-linear regression with span $= 0.6$. The observed value of the test statistic, $T^* = 0.597$, is larger than all 10,000 values.

and income in the Canadian occupational prestige data. This distribution is based on 10,000 random permutations of the data. The observed value of the test statistic is $T^* = 0.597$, a value that is larger than the Ts for all 10,000 randomly permuted data sets. The estimated p value for the randomization test is, therefore, $\hat{p} = 0/10,000 = 0$, essentially the same as the p value that we calculated for the standard F test of no relationship.

Permutation tests were first described by Fisher (1935) in his classic text on experimental design. The terminological distinction between *permutation tests* (all permutations of the data) and *randomization tests* (repeated random draws from the population of permutations) is not standard, but I find it useful. Further details on randomization and permutation tests may be found in Edgington (1987).

6. SPLINES*

Splines are piecewise polynomial functions that are constrained to join smoothly at points called *knots*. The traditional use of splines is for interpolation, but they can also be employed for parametric and nonparametric regression. Most applications employ cubic splines, the case that I shall consider here.

In addition to providing an alternative to local polynomial regression, the smoothing splines introduced in Section 6.2 are attractive as components of additive regression models, projection-pursuit regression, and generalized additive models, all described in the companion to this monograph (Fox, in press).

6.1. Regression Splines

One approach to simple-regression modeling is to fit a relatively high-degree polynomial in x,

$$y_i = \alpha + \beta_1 x_i + \beta_2 x_i^2 + \cdots + \beta_p x_i^p + \varepsilon_i$$

capable of capturing relationships of widely varying form. General polynomial fits, however, are highly nonlocal: As is familiar from least-

66

squares linear regression, data in one region can substantially affect the fit far away from that region. As well, estimates of high-degree polynomials are subject to substantial sampling variation. An illustration, employing a cubic polynomial for the regression of occupational prestige on income, appears in Figure 6.1(a). Here, the cubic fit does quite well, although the curve appears to decline artificially at the extreme right of the data.

As an alternative, we can partition the data into bins, fitting a different polynomial regression in each bin—a generalization of the idea of binning and averaging (described in Chapter 2). A defect of this procedure is that the curves fit to the different bins will almost surely be discontinuous, as illustrated for the occupational prestige data in Figure 6.1(b), using cubic regressions in two bins with a boundary at $10,000.

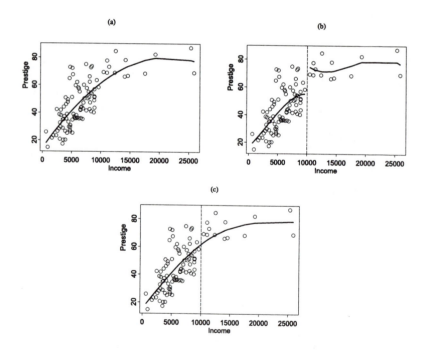

Figure 6.1. Polynomial fits to the Canadian occupational prestige data: (a) a global cubic fit; (b) independent cubic fits in two bins, divided at Income = 10,000; (c) a natural cubic spline, with one knot at Income = 10,000.

Cubic regression splines fit a third-degree polynomial in each bin under the added constraints that the curves join at the bin boundaries (the knots), and that the first and second derivatives (i.e., the slope and curvature of the regression function) are continuous at the knots. Matching the derivatives in this manner produces a smooth curve.

Natural cubic regression splines add knots at the boundaries of the data, and impose the additional condition that the fit is linear beyond the terminal knots. This requirement tends to avoid wild behavior near the extremes of the data. Suppose that there are k 'interior' knots and two knots at the boundaries, dividing the data into $k + 1$ bins. Each cubic regression uses four parameters, but there are three constraints at each interior knot,[14] and two additional constraints of linearity beyond the terminal knots, yielding in all $4(k+1) - 3k - 2 = k + 2$ independent parameters.

With the values of the knots fixed, a regression spline is just a linear model (i.e., can be fit by linear least-squares regression), and as such provides a fully parametric fit to the data. The practical difficulty in applying the method, however, is to decide how many knots are required, and where precisely they should be located.

Figure 6.1 (c) shows the result of fitting a natural cubic regression spline to the Canadian occupational prestige data. There is one knot at Income $= 10,000$, the location of which was determined by examining the scatterplot, and the model therefore uses only 3 parameters.

6.2. Smoothing Splines

In contrast to regression splines, *smoothing splines* arise as the solution to the following nonparametric-regression problem: Find the function $\widehat{f}(x)$ with two continuous derivatives that minimizes the *penalized sum of squares*,

$$SS^*(h) = \sum_{i=1}^{n}[y_i - f(x_i)]^2 + h \int_{x_{\min}}^{x_{\max}} [f''(x)]^2 \, dx \qquad (6.1)$$

where h is a smoothing constant, analogous to the bandwidth of a kernel or local-polynomial estimator.

• The first term in equation 6.1 is the residual sum of squares.

- The second term is a *roughness penalty*, which is large when the integrated second derivative of the regression function $f''(x)$ is large—that is, when $f(x)$ is rough. The endpoints of the integral enclose the data: $x_{min} < x_{(1)}$ and $x_{max} > x_{(n)}$.
- At one extreme, if the smoothing constant is set at $h = 0$ (and if all the x-values are distinct), then $\widehat{f}(x)$ simply interpolates the data.
- At the other extreme, if h is very large, then $\widehat{f}$ will be selected so that $\widehat{f}''(x)$ is everywhere 0, which implies a globally linear least-squares fit to the data.

It turns out, surprisingly and elegantly, that the function $\widehat{f}(x)$ that minimizes Equation 6.1 is a natural cubic spline with knots at the distinct observed values of x. Although this result seems to imply that n parameters are required (when all x-values are distinct), the roughness penalty imposes additional constraints on the solution, typically reducing the equivalent number of parameters for the smoothing spline substantially, and preventing $\widehat{f}(x)$ from interpolating the data. Indeed, it is common to select the smoothing constant h indirectly by setting the equivalent number of parameters for the smoother. An illustration appears in Figure 6.2, comparing a smoothing spline with a local-linear fit employing the same equivalent number of parameters (degrees of freedom). Precisely the same considerations arise in the

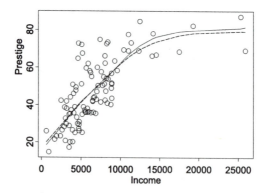

Figure 6.2. Nonparametric regression of occupational prestige on income, using local linear regression (solid line) and a smoothing spline (broken line), both with 4.3 equivalent parameters.

selection of h for smoothing splines as in the selection of the span for local polynomial smoothers (Sections 4.1 and 4.3).

Smoothing splines offer certain small advantages in comparison with local polynomial smoothers. Both smoothers are linear, in the sense that they can be written in the form $\widehat{\mathbf{y}} = \mathbf{Sy}$ for a suitably defined smoother matrix $\mathbf{S}$. The smoother matrix for smoothing splines is slightly better behaved, however, and if smoothing splines are employed as building blocks of an additive regression model, then the backfitting algorithm used to fit this model (as described in Fox, in press: chap. 3) is guaranteed to converge, a property that does not hold for the local polynomial smoother. On the negative side, smoothing splines do not generalize easily to multiple regression.

More information on smoothing splines may be found in a variety of sources, most notably Green and Silverman (1994); also see Hastie and Tibshirani (1990: sections 2.9–2.10).

6.3. Equivalent Kernels

One way of comparing linear smoothers like local polynomial estimators and smoothing splines, is to think of them as variants of the kernel estimator (Chapter 3), where fitted values arise as weighted averages of observed response values. This approach is illustrated in Figure 6.3, which shows *equivalent kernel weights* at two focal x-values in the Canadian occupational prestige data: One value, $x_{(5)}$, is near the boundary of the data; the other, $x_{(60)}$, is closer to the middle of the data. The figure shows tricube-kernel weights [panels (a) and (b)], along with the equivalent kernel weights for the local linear estimator with span = .6 (or 4.3 equivalent parameters) [panels (c) and (d)], and the smoothing spline with 4.3 equivalent parameters [in panels (e) and (f)].

All three estimators use similar kernels near the middle of the data, but the local linear estimator and the smoothing spline, while similar to each other, are quite different from the kernel estimator near the boundary. Recall that the kernel estimator can exhibit bias at the edge of the data when, as here, the regression has a large slope near the boundary. Note that the equivalent-kernel weights are generally asymmetric for local polynomial regression and for smoothing splines, and that some weights are negative.

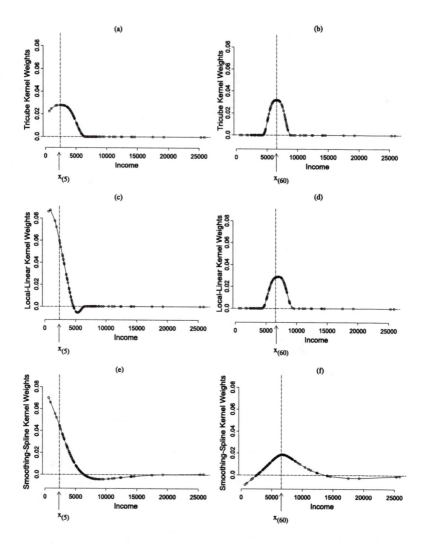

Figure 6.3. Equivalent kernels for three nonparametric estimators of the regression of occupational prestige on income: (a) and (b) nearest-neighbor tricube kernel estimator, with span = .6; (c) and (d) nearest-neighbor local-linear estimator, with span = .6 (4.3 equivalent parameters); (e) and (f) smoothing spline, with 4.3 equivalent parameters. The focal point, marked by an arrow, is $x_{(5)}$ in (a), (c), and (e), and $x_{(60)}$ in (b), (d), and (f).

7. NONPARAMETRIC REGRESSION AND DATA ANALYSIS

The scatterplot is the most important data-analytic statistical graph (see, e.g., Jacoby, 1997). I am tempted to suggest that you add a nonparametric-regression curve to every scatterplot that you draw, since the curve will help to reveal the relationship between the two variables in the plot. This advice is exaggerated—some scatterplots, such as quantile-comparison plots, do not require smoothing—but it is not far off the mark.

Because scatterplots are adaptable to so many different contexts in data analysis, it is not possible to survey their uses exhaustively here. Instead, I shall concentrate on an issue closely related to nonparametric regression: detecting and dealing with nonlinearity. The possibility of nonlinearity is omnipresent in multiple-regression analysis as it is in simple regression. One response is to employ nonparametric multiple regression, as described in the companion to this monograph (Fox, in press). An alternative is to fit a preliminary linear regression, to employ appropriate diagnostic plots to detect departures from linearity, and to follow up by specifying a new parametric model that captures nonlinearity detected in the diagnostics, for example by transforming a predictor.

7.1. The "Bulging Rule"

The first example in this monograph examined the relationship between the infant-mortality rates and GDP per capita of 193 nations of the world. A scatterplot of the data supplemented by a local-linear regression, in Figure 1.1(a), reveals a highly nonlinear relationship between the two variables: Infant mortality declines smoothly with GDP, but at a rapidly decreasing rate. Taking the logarithms of the two variables, in Figure 1.1(b), renders the relationship nearly linear.

Mosteller and Tukey (1977) suggested a systematic rule—which they call the *"bulging rule"*—for selecting linearizing transformations from the family of powers and roots, where a variable x is replaced by the power x^p. For example, when $p = 2$, the variable is replaced by its square, x^2; when $p = -1$, the variable is replaced by its inverse, $x^{-1} = 1/x$; when $p = 1/2$, the variable is replaced by its square root, $x^{1/2} = \sqrt{x}$; and so on. The only exception we make to this straightforward definition is that $p = 0$ designates the log transformation, $\log x$, rather than the 0th power.[14] We are not constrained to pick simple values of p, but doing so often aids interpretation.

Transformations in the family of powers and roots are applicable only when all of the values of x are positive: Some of the transformations, such as square root and log, are undefined for negative values of x. Other transformations, such as x^2, would distort the order of x if some x values are negative and some are positive. A simple solution is to use a "start"—to add a constant quantity c to all values of x prior to applying the power transformation: $x \rightarrow (x+c)^p$. Notice that negative powers—such as the inverse transformation, x^{-1}—reverse the order of the x values. If we want to preserve the original order, then we can take $x \rightarrow -x^p$ when p is negative.

Power transformation of x or y can help linearize a nonlinear relationship that is both *simple* and *monotone*. What is meant by these terms is illustrated in Figure 7.1:

- A relationship is simple in the present context when it is smoothly curved and when the curvature does not change direction.
- A relationship is monotone when y strictly increases or decreases with x.

Thus, the relationship in Figure 7.1(a) is simple and monotone; the relationship in Figure 7.1(b) is monotone but not simple, because the direction of curvature changes from opening up to opening down; and the relationship in Figure 7.1(c) is simple but *non*monotone, because y first decreases and then increases with x.

Although nonlinear relationships that are not simple or that are nonmonotone cannot be linearized by a power transformation, other forms of parametric regression may be applicable. For example, the relationship in Figure 7.1(c) could be modeled as a quadratic equation in x:

$$y = \alpha + \beta_1 x + \beta_2 x^2 + \varepsilon.$$

Polynomial regression models, such as quadratic equations, can be fitted by linear least squares regression. Nonlinear least squares can be used to fit an even broader class of parametric models (see, e.g., Fox, 1997, sect. 14.2).

(a)

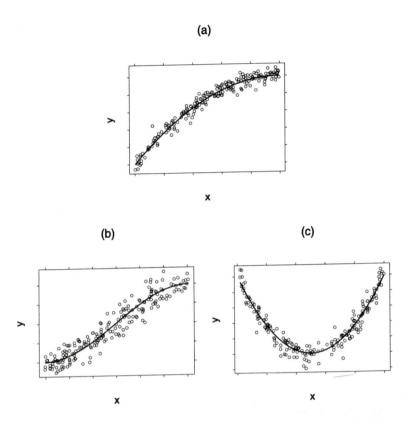

(b)

(c)

Figure 7.1. The relationship in (a) is simple and monotone, that in (b) is montone but not simple, and that in (c) is simple but nonmonotone. Power transformations of x or y can serve to linearize the relationship in (a), but not in (b) or (c).

Mosteller and Tukey's bulging rule is illustrated in Figure 7.2: When, as in the infant-mortality data of Figure 1.1(a), the bulge points *down* and to the *left*, the relationship is linearized by moving x "*down* the ladder" of powers and roots toward $\sqrt{x}$, $\log x$, and $1/x$, or by moving y *down* the ladder of powers and roots, or both. When the bulge points *up*, we can move x *up* the ladder of powers toward x^2 and x^3; when the bulge points to the *right*, we can move y *up* the ladder of powers. Specific linearizing transformations are located by trial and error; the farther one moves from no trans-

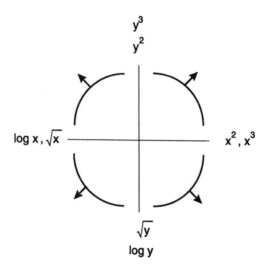

Figure 7.2. Mosteller and Tukey's bulging rule for locating a linearizing trans-formation. The direction of the bulge indicates whether to move *x* or *y* up or down the ladder of powers and roots. Specific transformations are selected by trial and error.

formation, corresponding to $p = 1$, the greater the effect of the transformation.

In the example, log transformations of both infant mortality and GDP somewhat overcorrect the original nonlinearity, producing a small bulge pointing up and to the right. Nevertheless, the nonlin-earity in the transformed data is relatively slight, and using log trans-formations for both variables yields a simple interpretation. The least squares line plotted in Figure 1.1(b) has the equation

$$\log_{10} (\text{InfantMortality}) = 3.06 - 0.493 \times \log_{10} \text{GDP}.$$

The slope of this relationship, $b = -0.493$, is what economists call an *elasticity*: On average, a 1% increase in GDP per capita is associated with an approximate $\frac{1}{2}$% decline in the infant-mortality rate.

7.2. Partial-Residual Plots

Suppose that y is additively, but not necessarily linearly, related to $x_1, x_2, \ldots, x_k$, so that

$$y_i = \alpha + f_1(x_{1i}) + f_2(x_{2i}) + \cdots + f_k(x_{ki}) + \varepsilon_i.$$

If the *partial-regression function* f_j is simple and monotone, then we can use the bulging rule to find a transformation that linearizes the partial relationship between y and the predictor x_j. Alternatively, if f_j takes the form of a simple polynomial in x_j, such as a quadratic or cubic, then we can specify a parametric model containing polynomial terms in that predictor.

Discovering nonlinearity in multiple regression is intrinsically more difficult than in simple regression because the predictors typically are correlated. The scatterplot of y against x_j, therefore, is informative about the *marginal* relationship between these variables, ignoring the other predictors, but is not necessarily informative about the *partial* relationship f_j of y to x_j, holding the other xs constant.

Under relatively broad circumstances (see Cook, 1998, chap. 14; Cook & Weisberg, 1994, chap. 9; Fox, 1997, sect. 12.3.2), *partial-residual plots* (also called *component+residual plots*) can help to detect nonlinearity in multiple regression. Let us fit a preliminary linear least squares regression,

$$y_i = a + b_1 x_{1i} + b_2 x_{2i} + \cdots + b_k x_{ki} + e_i.$$

Then, to form the *partial residuals* for x_j, add the least squares residuals to the linear component of the relationship between y and x_j:

$$e_{i(j)} = e_i + b_j x_{ji}.$$

The essential idea here is that an unmodeled nonlinear component of the relationship between y and x_j should appear in the least squares residuals, so that plotting and smoothing $e_{(j)}$ against x_j will reveal the partial relationship between y and x_j. We think of the smoothed partial-residual plot as an estimate $\widehat{f_j}$ of the partial-regression function. This procedure is repeated for each predictor, $j = 1, 2, \ldots, k$.

Illustrative partial-residual plots for the regression of prestige on income and education in the Canadian occupational prestige data appear in Figure 7.3. The solid line on each plot gives a local-linear fit;

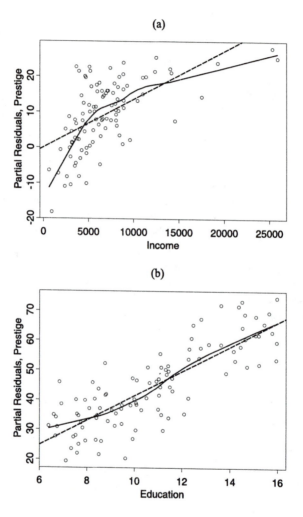

Figure 7.3. Partial-residual plots for the regression of occupational prestige on (a) income and (b) education. A local-linear fit, using span = 0.6, is drawn on each plot, along with the linear least squares line.

the broken line gives the linear least squares fit and represents the least squares multiple-regression plane viewed edge-on in the direction of the corresponding predictor.

- It is apparent from Figure 7.3(a) that the partial relationship between prestige and income, controlling for education, is substantially nonlinear. Although the nonparametric-regression curve is not altogether smooth, the bulge points up and to the left, suggesting transforming income down the ladder of powers and roots. Visual trial and error indicates that the log transformation of income serves to straighten the relationship between prestige and income. Unless all of the partial-residual plots show a similar pattern, we prefer, in multiple regression, to transform the predictor rather than the response variable, because transforming y will change its relationship to all of the xs.
- Figure 7.3(b) suggests that the partial relationship between prestige and education is nonlinear and monotone, but not simple. Consequently, a power transformation of education is not promising. We could try specifying a cubic regression for education (that is, including education, education^2, and education^3 in the regression model), but the departure from linearity is slight, and a viable alternative here is simply to treat the education effect as linear.

Regressing occupational prestige on education and the log (base 2) of income produces the result

$$\widehat{\text{prestige}} = -95.2 + 7.93 \times \log_2 \text{income} + 4.00 \times \text{education}.$$

Thus, holding education constant and doubling income (i.e., increasing $\log_2$ income by 1) is associated, on average, with an increment in prestige of about 8 points; holding income constant and increasing education by 1 year is associated, on average, with an increment in prestige of 4 points.

7.3. Concluding Remarks

Nonparametric multiple regression (described in Fox, in press) can *replace* the more familiar linear least squares multiple regression in many applications. Nonparametric generalized regression (also described in Fox, in press) extends these methods to binary data, count data, and so on. The cost of nonparametric multiple regression is a substantially increased burden of computation and greater difficulty of interpretation. The potential gain is enhanced fidelity to the data.

In contrast, nonparametric simple regression—the subject of the current monograph—is best regarded as a *supplement* to other statistical methods (as illustrated in its application to partial-residual plots and choice of linearizing transformations in regression) and as a precursor to nonparmetric multiple regression. Nevertheless, the ubiquity of scatterplots in data analysis and the wide availability of software for scatterplot smoothing make the potential range of application of nonparametric simple regression very broad.

NOTES

1. The curvilinear relationship between labor-force participation and log estimated wages is probably an artifact of the construction of the estimated wage rates: For women who were working, the estimated wage was taken as their actual remuneration. A regression equation fit to the data for working women was used to predict the wage rates for those who were not working outside of the home. Because the predictions have no residual component, they are less variable than actual wage rates, producing fewer extreme scores and inducing a curvlinear relationship between labor-force participation and wage rate. The linear logistic regressions in Berndt (1991) and Long (1997) employ additional predictors, but suffer from the same problem.

2. Ordering the x values is not strictly necessary here, but it facilitates connecting the fitted values into the estimated regression curve.

3. It is possible that $\overline{\mu} = \mu \mid x_0$ by good fortune, for example, but this is an unusual occurrence.

4. I am using the term "bias" slightly loosely here, because we are examining the performance of each of these estimators for a *particular* sample, rather than averaged over *all* samples, but the point is nevertheless valid.

5. These formulas are derived in Bowman and Azzalini (1997, pp. 72–73). The two constants are

$$s_K^2 = \int z^2 K(z)\, dz,$$

$$a_K^2 = \int [K(z)]^2\, dz.$$

If the kernel $K(z)$ is a probability density function symmetric around 0, such as the standard normal distribution, then s_K^2 is the variance of this distribution For the standard normal kernel, for example, $s_K^2 = 1$ and $a_K^2 = 0.282$. For the tricube kernel (which is not a density function), $s_K^2 = 1/6$ and $a_K^2 = 0.949$.

6. The expected effective sample size contributing to the estimate at $x = x_0$ is proportional to $nhp(x_0)$, the denominator of the variance.

7. Alternatively, rather than averaging over the observed x values, we could integrate over the probability density of x, producing the mean integrated square error (MISE):

$$\text{MISE}(s) = \int \left\{ E[\hat{y} \mid x(s)] - \mu \mid x \right\} p(x)\, dx.$$

We can think of MASE as a discrete version of MISE.

8. This formula follows from more general results given in Simonoff (1996, sect. 5.5.2).

9. The local-quadratic regression provides a somewhat neater example for these data than the local-linear fit. Although asymptotically the local-cubic estimator has an advantage over the local-quadratic estimator (as explained in Section 4.2), this advantage is not necessarily obtained in a small sample, and the software employed (the loess function in S-plus) provides only for linear and quadratic fits.

10. I have used the generalized additive modeling package in S-Plus (Hastie, 1992; Hastie & Tibshirani, 1990) for these computations.

11. The applicability of the bootstrap to this illustration is questionable, since the 102 occupations are not a random sample of the larger group of occupations to which one might wish to draw inferences. The variability of estimates is still arguably of interest, however, because it allows us to assess the extent to which patterns observed in the data could have been the product of chance. Moreover, the issue is not unique to the bootstrap—it applies equally to traditional procedures for statistical inference.

12. We could equivalently use the F statistic from Equation 5.3.

13. How many random permutations are required? Let p denote the permutation-test p value (from Equation 5.6) and let $\hat{p}$ represent the estimate of the p value based on m randomly selected permutations. Because $\hat{p}$ is a sample proportion, its standard error is

$$SE(\hat{p}) = \sqrt{\frac{p(1-p)}{m}}.$$

Suppose that $p = 0.05$, for example, and that we are content with a standard error of 0.005. Then we require

$$m = \frac{p(1-p)}{[SE(\hat{p})]^2} = \frac{0.05(1-0.05)}{0.005^2} = 1900$$

random permutations. This calculation is rough because the distribution of $\hat{p}$ is neither normal nor symmetric when p is close to 0.

14. Recall that the pieces of the spline are constrained to join at the interior knots, and to have the same first and second derivatives on either side of each interior knot.

15. Literally applying the 0th power would be useless, because to do so would change x to a constant, $x^0 = 1$. The log transformation behaves like a 0th power in the sense that as p gets very close to 0, the quantity $(x^p - 1)/p$ gets very close to $\log x$. (The subtraction of 1 and the division by p here are inessential, because they just linearly transform x^p.)

REFERENCES

BERNDT, E. R. (1991). *The Practice of Econometrics: Classic and Contemporary*. Reading, MA: Addison-Wesley.

BLISHEN, B. R., and McROBERTS, H. A. (1976). A revised socioeconomic index for occupations in Canada. *Canadian Review of Sociology and Anthropology*, 13, 71–79.

BOWMAN, A. W., and AZZALINI, A. (1997). *Applied Smoothing Techniques for Data Analysis: The Kernel Approach with S-Plus Illustrations*. Oxford, UK: University Press.

CLEVELAND, W. S. (1979). Robust locally weighted regression and smoothing scatterplots. *Journal of the American Statistical Association*, 74, 829–836.

CLEVELAND, W. S., GROSSE, E., and SHYU, W. M. (1992). Local regression models. In J. M. Chambers and T. J. Hastie, (Eds.), *Statistical Models in S*, (pp. 309–376). Pacific Grove, CA: Wadsworth and Brooks/Cole.

COOK, R. D. (1998). *Regression Graphics: Ideas for Studying Regressions Through Graphics*. New York: Wiley.

COOK, R. D., and WEISBERG, S. (1994). *An Introduction to Regression Graphics*. New York: Wiley.

EDGINGTON, E. S. (1987). *Randomization Tests* (2nd ed.). New York: Dekker.

EFRON, B., and TIBSHIRANI, R. J. (1993). *An Introduction to the Bootstrap*. New York: Chapman and Hall.

FISHER, R. A. (1935). *Design of Experiments*. Edinburgh: Oliver and Boyd.

FOX, J. (1991). *Regression Diagnostics* (Sage University Paper series on Quantitative Applications in the Social Sciences, series no. 07-79). Newbury Park, CA: Sage.

FOX, J. (1997). *Applied Regression Analysis, Linear Models, and Related Methods*. Thousand Oaks, CA: Sage.

FOX, J. (in press). *Generalized and Multiple Nonparametric Regression*. Thousand Oaks, CA: Sage.

GREEN, P. J., and SILVERMAN, B. W. (1994). *Nonparametric Regression and Generalized Linear Models: A Roughness Penalty Approach*. London: Chapman and Hall.

HASTIE, T. J. (1992). Generalized additive models. In J. M. Chambers and T. J. Hastie (Eds.), *Statistical Models in S* (pp. 249–307). Pacific Grove, CA: Wadsworth and Brooks/Cole.

HASTIE, T. J., and TIBSHIRANI, R. J. (1990). *Generalized Additive Models*. London: Chapman and Hall.

JACOBY, W. G. (1997). *Statistical Graphics for Univariate and Bivariate Data* (Sage University Paper series on Quantitative Applications in the Social Sciences, series no. 07-117). Thousand Oaks, CA: Sage.

LEINHARDT, S., and WASSERMAN, S. S. (1978). Exploratory data analysis: An introduction to selected methods. In K. F. Schuessler (Ed.), *Sociological Methodology 1979* (pp. 311–365). San Francisco: Jossey-Bass.

LONG, J. S. (1997). *Regression Models for Categorical and Limited Dependent Variables.* Thousand Oaks, CA: Sage.

MCCULLAGH, P., and NELDER, J. A. (1989). *Generalized Linear Models* (2nd ed.). London: Chapman and Hall.

MOONEY, C. Z., and DUVAL, R. D. (1993). *Bootstrapping: A Nonparametric Approach to Statistical Inference* (Sage University Paper series on Quantitative Applications in the Social Sciences, series no. 07-95). Newbury Park, CA: Sage.

MOSTELLER, F., and TUKEY, J. W. (1977). *Data Analysis and Regression.* Reading, MA: Addison-Wesley.

MROZ, T. A. (1987). The sensitivity of an emprical model of married women's hours of work to economic and statistical assumptions. *Econometrica*, 55, 765–799.

OSTROM, Jr., C. W. (1990). *Time Series Analysis: Regression Techniques* (2nd ed.) (Sage University Paper series on Quantitative Applications in the Social Sciences, series no. 07-9). Newbury Park, CA: Sage.

SIMONOFF, J. S. (1996). *Smoothing Methods in Statistics.* New York: Springer-Verlag.

STINE, R. (1990). An introduction to bootstrap methods: Examples and ideas. In J. Fox and J. S. Long (Eds.), *Modern Methods of Data Analysis* (pp. 325–373). Newbury Park, CA: Sage.

TUKEY, J. W. (1977). *Exploratory Data Analysis.* Reading, MA: Addison-Wesley.

United Nations (1998). Social indicators. Available at {http://www.un.org/Depts/unsd/social/main.htm}.

VENABLES, W. N., and RIPLEY, B. D. (1997). *Modern Applied Statistics with S-PLUS* (2nd ed). New York: Springer-Verlag.

ABOUT THE AUTHOR

John Fox is Professor of Sociology at McMaster University in Hamilton, Ontario, Canada. He has written and lectured widely on social statistics. Professor Fox is the author of an earlier monograph on *Regression Diagnostics* (Sage, 1991) in the QASS series and of *Applied Regression Analysis, Linear Models, and Related Methods* (Sage, 1997). His recent and current research includes work on polls in the 1995 Quebec sovereignty referendum and the 1997 Canadian federal election, and experiments on the perception of three-dimensional dynamic statistical graphs.